MW00953402

THE DEFINITIVE GUIDE FOR SOLVING BIBLICAL QUESTIONS ABOUT MARY:

Mary Among the Evangelists

Biblical Dogmatics Vol. 1

By Rev. Dr. Christiaan Kappes & William Albrecht

Patristic Pillars Press
1534 Eidson Rd, Suite B
Eagle Pass, Texas 78852
www.PatristicPillars.com

Contents

Dedications

This work is dedicated to Fr. Peter Damian Fehlner, OFM, whose life was spent in virtue rooted in his mastery of St. Bonaventure of Bagnoregio's and Bl. John Duns Scotus's saintly lives and erudition in theology, particularly on Mary. This volume is the fruit of the lessons from the least of his sons in both of the aforementioned disciplines but his disciple nonetheless hopes that his love for his master and his master's love for all things honoring the mother of the Savior might somehow redound to Fr. Peter's glory on earth as he already enjoys it in heaven, where he rests with the woman "higher than than Seraphim and beyond compare more honorable than the Cherubim, who a virgin gave birth to God the Word. You truly, o Theotokos, we magnify!"

-Rev. Dr. Christiaan Kappes

For Olivia, may our Theotokos lead you to Christ.

-William

Endorsements

"The mystery of the Virgin Mary is integral to the Gospels, not added. The earliest Christians knew this. I'm very pleased that someone has finally taken up the task of undoing the damage wreaked by generations of misdirected academics. A systematic study of the gospels and the patristic sources, like this one, is long overdue. Tradition is vindicated in these pages." - **Dr. Scott Hahn** holds the Father Michael Scanlan, T.O.R., Chair of Biblical Theology and the New Evangelization at Franciscan University of Steubenville, and is the founder and president of the Saint Paul Center for Biblical Theology.

"A very impressive and insightful close reading of the NT passages concerning Mary using the good Jewish and Patristic principle of interpreting Scripture by means of Scripture. This book should prove very helpful to many readers and I hope it will be widely read." - **Dr. Sebastian Brock** is generally acknowledged as the foremost and most influential academic in the field of Syriac language today. He is widely known as today's leading scholar in Syriac Biblical and Patristic studies, and is known worldwide for his contributions to Near Eastern Studies.

"Few books on Mariology make true advancements in the field. Fr. Kappes and William Albrecht has done just that in their book, *The Definitive Guide for Solving Biblical Questions about Mary: Mary and the Evangelist.* The book contains a treasure trove of material and insights concerning the Scriptural and patristic roots of Marian doctrine. I highly recommend this book to anyone who is interested in gaining a deeper knowledge about the Blessed Virgin Mary." - **Gary Michuta** is one of the top Catholic Authors, Apologists, and Speakers. He is the radio host of the renowned Hands on Apologetics.

"Why another book on Mary? First, Mary and Marian studies are fascinating and often controversial; they never exhaust our interest. Second, this book answers questions in a new and insightful way digging deep into Scripture and Tradition with fresh eyes, revealing profound and astute discoveries. Fr. Kappes and William Albrecht clarify and simplify many a conundrum enabling Catholics to have a clear and cogent response to theological challenges and to inspire a fresh love and devotion to the Blessed Virgin and her Son. Easy to approach for the novice, yet a scholarly and fresh read for the expert." - **Steve Ray** is a top Catholic speaker, author, pilgrimage guide, and frequent guest on EWTN, Virgin Most Powerful Radio, and Reason & Theology.

"The evangelists gave Mary her proper place in the Gospels, and the Fathers of the first millennium honored it. Interpreters since the Reformation have tried to remove her. This book is a great act of restoration, justice. and piety." - **Mike Aquilina** is the award-winning author of more than forty books on Catholic history, doctrine, and devotion.

Introduction

From the most ancient of days, Christians believed that the Scriptures held a very special place in their everyday worship. The Scripture, for the Ancient Church, was inspired by God, and able to prepare each one for good works (2 Timothy 3:17). The apostles and followers of Christ vouchsafed the truth of Holy Writ, passing on the fiery truth of God's holy word as one handing on a never vanquishing torch, to those faithful adherents that followed in their footsteps. St. Paul firmly believed that the fulfillment of the faith had come in the very foundation of the Church that Jesus Christ established with its visible hierarchy. He also recognized that the importance of Holy Writ was one that was firmly entrenched in the infant Church, which received it from the divinely inspired traditions of the Jews (Romans 3:2). In the Hebrew Scriptures, the divinely inspired authors laid a foundation that served as the very edifice upon which the later authors of the Greek Old and New Testaments leaned. In several books which Catholics fondly call Deuterocanonicals, you see the authors providing the ancient and traditional God-inspired interpretations of texts that came before their time. Such a trend was not merely confined to the Greek Old Testament which we call the Septuagint, but was also found within the Hebrew Scriptures themselves. It is no surprise then, that St. Paul was able to explain that all of Holy Writ is actually God-breathed or *theopneustos*. [1] Such a standard for canonicity was one that the earliest Christians knew quite well. What we will encounter in this first chapter is a clear portrait of the Virgin Mary, in the very minds and hearts of the Evangelists Matthew and Mark. It is our hope that readers will be able to realize fully why much ink was spilt by the early martyrs and pillars of the faith. The ancient Christians, who were handed on the torch of everlasting truth, were able to find clarity in the Gospels. So, we shall approach such important and purportedly difficult passages with the desire to understand how the first Christians that walked hallowed lands would have understood them. Today, we frequently hear the claim that James, Joses, Judas, Simon, and the sisters that are listed in the Gospels, were actually the blood relatives of Jesus Christ from his mother Mary. But, was this the

---

[1] For the significance of St. Paul's use of this word, see Max Zerwick and Mary Grosvenor, *A grammatical analysis of the Greek New Testament* (Rome: Biblical Institute Press, 1974), 644.

belief of that foundation of truth that the great Ignatius dubbed the Catholic Church in which Jesus himself was said to be present? [2]

Were these "relatives" the actual children of Mary from Joseph? We will see that allowing the evangelist Mark to unveil his own interpretation will be the key in understanding his Gospel, and the underlying message of salvation history present therein. The lover of the Scriptures will feel satiated at seeing the conclusions of this study, for as the ultimate identities of these figures are clearly unveiled. The reader will gain a deeper appreciation for how Mark and Matthew so seamlessly weave their historical events together, and how the early church Fathers were able to interpret their masterful language, in which they preserved the inspired truth of the word of God. The introductory study in chapter 1, as we will see, does not conclude after we lift the veil on these characters' identities, but rather segue ways perfectly into the good news of St. Matthew's Gospel account. Matthew so expertly hearkens to the Septuagint rendering of Isaiah chapter 7, where the sacred author so ably defends and promotes the truth of the Virgin, conceiving and giving birth in virginity, a prophecy that was foretold by the prophet Isaiah: "Therefore the Lord himself will give you this sign: the virgin shall be with child, and bear a son, and shall name him Immanuel" (Isaiah 7:14). Matthew's masterful tome leads us to the all-important "until" verse, which is found in the first chapter: "When Joseph woke from sleep, he did as the angel of the Lord commanded him; he took his wife, but knew her not, *until* she had borne a son; and he called his name Jesus" (Matthew 1:24-25).

For many years, Catholics have arrived at the end of Matthew's first chapter of his Gospel, and have readied themselves to spill much ink defending the perpetual virginity of Mary, by providing a cogent defense of how the Greek "until" can mean a continuation of an action or a state beyond the time stated in said text. But, perhaps it's possible to reach a conclusion by examining the very Scripture contained within the Scripture of Matthew itself! Is it possible that the solution to this supposed problem was found by reading the text with "ancient" lenses? Is it possible that the very lenses that we perhaps allude to were the very manner in which the most ancient of Christians read the Bible itself? We will find that one of the most eloquent of the Greek speaking Church Fathers, St. John Chrysostom, confirms the very heart and core of our very first chapter. Where Chrysostom serves as the confirmation of our thesis, the erudite pillar of

---

[2] Michael Holmes, *The Apostolic Fathers: Greek texts and English translations* (Grand Rapids, MI: Baker Books, 1999), 191.

14

apologetics and Biblical translations himself, St. Jerome, ably confirms how the very Gospel accounts themselves provide such sharp clarity, that one is fully able to understand how the core Marian doctrines are not only able to be defended from Holy Writ, but are defined in the very Scripture, which we thoroughly and adequately examine. When St. Athanasius stood as a stalwart defender of orthodoxy against the heretical Arians, he famously said that the Scriptures worked in a fantastic and harmonious manner, able to reveal the very truths that God intended them to illuminate to the faithful lovers of truth.[3] The reader's journey through chapter 1 will provide clarity on the extremely important figure known as the Virgin Mary, and it is our hope to emulate St. Paul who so masterfully stated to St. Titus that one must have a solid and firm grasp of the inerrant word so as to be able to preach doctrine and correct common misunderstandings (Titus 1:9).

Crossing the threshold of our second chapter, we reach the incredible historian, St. Luke[4] who in some ways wrote in a style of the Greek Titan of history, Thucydides. Luke's gospel has frequently been dubbed the Marian Gospel. Indeed, it was the late Rev. Dr. Brown who mused as to what St. Luke's sources were for his gospel account.[5] Our goal that (we have undertaken) is to approach the saintly doctor's Scripturally rich text as a first century Greek-speaking Christian would have. It is abundantly clear that it was indeed Mary who served as the witness (that St. Luke interviewed) for information about the Holy Spirit's overshadowing of her, as well as the birth and life of Christ in his infancy[6] Luke is clear that we are supposed to be *hypêretai*, or servants, of the very word (Luke

---

[3] Athanasius of Alexandria, *Festal Letters*, in *St. Athanasius: Select Works and Letters*, ed. Philip Schaff and Henry Wace, trans. H. Burgess and J. Smith Payne (New York: Christian Literature Company, 1892), 4:546.

[4] For insights into Luke's style and paradigms, see T. M. Troftgruben, *Luke as Historian*, in *The Lexham Bible Dictionary*, ed. J. D. Barry, D. Bomar, et al. (Bellingham WA: Lexham Press, 2016).

[5] Raymond Brown, *The Birth of the Messiah: A Commentary on the Infancy Narratives in the Gospels of Matthew and Luke*, 2nd ed (New York: Yale University Press, 1993), 622.

[6] Arthur Just, *Luke* (Downers Grove, IL: InterVarsity Press, 2005), 3:25.

1:2).[7] Luke works as a masterful artist, painting a portrait of texts in the Greek Old Testament to his current day. Luke's strong Marian emphasis was also captured within the Early Church. It is here where our unique insight into the world of the first Christians takes a very special approach. We are able to get a glimpse into the mind of the earliest Fathers of the Faith that were clear and steadfast in their belief that it was indeed the Virgin Mary who was the one who heard the word and kept it, treasuring it in the very depths of her heart for all of her life. Let the reader join us through this journey as we witness St. Zechariah's rejection of that prophetic word and Mary's vouchsafing of the eternal truth of Holy Writ. It is our heartfelt desire that the reader become showered by the all-encompassing riches of the Scriptures, where we realize that for our omnipotent God, nothing is "too wonderful"! It is here in our in-depth analysis where Scripture begins to truly unfold like never before. Here we see that "Angel" from the Old Testament theophanies become incarnate as(so-called Mister) Wonderful in the womb of the Virgin. It is also here where typology and prophecy interconnect to show how the portrait Luke lays out for us slowly begins to materialize before our very eyes. With each stroke of his saintly pen, he shows us how the Virgin Birth and Mary as perpetual virgin are Scriptural and historical! It is here that we have undertaken the task to lay out five major tiers to fully bring out the beauty of the Christian faith. With each page you turn, Scripture and the Fathers slowly bring to life the holy air that Luke breathed in the presence of our Blessed Mother, as she recounted these truths to him. From Genesis, to Judges, to the Prophet Samuel, the reader will get a clearer understanding of the fulfillment of the Virgin Birth and Mary's holy vow of perpetual virginity. The inspired word of God will guide our reader throughout the tour of the blessed roads Luke traversed as he conversed with his eyewitnesses. It is our desire that before encountering chapter 3, the reader be illuminated by Hannah's amazing annunciation, and that the same reader be filled with a desire to venerate the Virgin's purity, as Luke's pen strokes bring out the beauty of Mary as the New Ark of the Covenant.

Chapter 3 follows St. Luke as he shows his adeptness for the Greek texts of the Old Testament. St. Jerome noted how Luke was especially skilled in his

---

[7] For references to the Greek edition of the New Testament, see Kurt Aland, M. Black, et al. (ed.), *The Greek New Testament, Fourth Revised Edition (with Morphology)* (Stuttgart: Deutsche Bibelgesellschaft, 2006).

usage of eloquent Biblical Greek.[8] Acting as an inimitable historian, he presents to us one of the greatest historical events in history, in the Annunciation of our Blessed Virgin in a most stunning manner. In our presentation to our readers of these magnificent teachings that Luke has preserved and put forth, we pilfer the Patristic archives to show that these teachings were indeed recognized as crucial and ancient for the first followers of the faith. Rev. Dr. Brown notices ancient material that Luke is hearkening to for what he ultimately recognizes as the divine prophetic fulfillments in the first chapter of Luke and beyond, but unfortunately fails to connect some vitally important Scriptures that were clear to the ancient Church and of which St. Luke was well aware, with the result that he saw divine fulfillment come to true fruition in his portrait of the Virgin.[9] It is our belief that the reader will gain a deeper appreciation for the Biblical Mary, a deeper reverence for the "Hail Mary", as readers can see the Lucan theological system unveiled before their very eyes. Where Rev. Dr. Brown failed to see Mary as the true icon of Zion,[10] we connect the Biblical and ancient view, which clearly portrays the Virgin as that image of not only the New Zion, but Jerusalem, and even the faithful remnant of Judah. Perhaps even more fascinating to the lover of all of Holy Writ, our examination of Luke's record brings us to the fascinating Deuterocanonical book of Sirach. It is well documented that St. Luke quoted from several Septuagint (LXX) books throughout his writings, and frequently relied on Sirach all throughout his written record.[11] Also known as the Book of Ecclesiasticus, Sirach was written in second century BC[12] and was utilized as Holy Writ by the earliest Christians. It is this very book that was famously condemned by Rabbi Akiba as having been one of the foremost texts that the early Church utilized for prophecies of Christ that had been fulfilled in the New Testament era.

---

[8] Jerome, *Lives of Illustrious Men*, in *Theodoret, Jerome, Gennadius, Rufinus: Historical Writings, etc.*, ed. Philip Schaff and H. Wace, trans. Ernest Cushing Richardson (New York: Christian Literature Company, 1892), 3:363.

[9] Brown, *The Birth of the Messiah*, 629.

[10] Ibid., 320.

[11] For a study on the question, see D. A. Jones, *Old Testament Quotations and Allusions in the New Testament* (Bellingham, WA: Logos Bible Software, 2009).

[12] Jason Kuo, *Book of Sirach*, in *The Lexham Bible Dictionary*, ed. J. D. Barry, D. Bomar, et al. (Bellingham, WA: Lexham Press, 2016).

We undertake the task to show how Luke "graced" us with his connection of Sirach, chapter 18, into the very text of Luke chapter 1, where the Greek *kecharitômenê* is used to show that Mary is "full of grace". Reginald Garrigou-Lagrange famously noted on more than one occasion that Mary's filling with grace, so notable in this passage, was one of absolutely important significance.[13] The ever-meticulous Lucan artistry is appreciated for its finely woven strokes of wisdom in his identification of Mary as the New Daughter of Jephthah and thus, the New Ark of the Covenant. Together with us, we hope that the reader's journey is as incredulous as Mary's moment of joy and shock at Gabriel's announcing the coming of the Messiah, indeed, the so-called (by us) Mr. Wonderful, in her very womb. Mary's vow of remaining a virgin her whole life is one that is well founded in Scripture and the Church Fathers. We will see how the most erudite figures of Christendom interpreted these passages in this long forgotten traditional manner. The belief that Mary remained a virgin her whole life was one that was strongly believed and held to by the Golden-Age Church Fathers, as well as by the very first Protestant Reformers. As we will see, through our trip through the Biblical world, what Basil of Caesarea called the "lovers of Christ" would deem the idea of Mary having had children at a point in her life as something so far from the realms of truth, that these musings would not have been embraced by the trained theologians and philosophers of the day. Through our in-depth study and examination of the cultural and supernatural world in which St. Luke enveloped himself, we come to realize how so very vital to Mary as Mother of God, was her virginity as that New Ark of the Covenant. Where modern day scholarship proved unable to connect every single dot of the ancient Christian world that grasped what Luke was saying, we undertook the task of connecting the clearly prophetic message of the Apostle and showed how it was without a doubt what he himself was asserting in this fulfillment of the Greek texts in the Old Testament Scriptures regarding our Blessed Mother. Indeed, so important to the Early Church was the very life of Mary that it became intertwined with Mary as Ark of the New Covenant with the result that the Fathers connected every part of Mary's life with her as that special Ark of God. Indeed it is the Dormition and Assumption narratives that are so strong in their emphasis on the Ark entering into heaven upon the end of Mary's earthly life. That holy Ark, where the Angels and Saints dance and celebrate its arrival into heaven, was described as none other than Holy Mary. The Fathers were

---

[13] Aidan Nichols, *There Is No Rose: The Mariology of the Catholic Church* (Minneapolis MN: Fortress Press, 2015), 103.

not shy to quote from the Lucan texts and the Scriptures upon which Luke so heavily relied to bring his Biblical world of fulfilled prophecy to life.

Having reached the finale of our delving into the mind and world of the Evangelists, we will have covered Biblical figures and typology perhaps long lost to history. Mary's hymn from the sterile Hannah will be revisited and reformulated. The crucial nature of this theology is not lost on us, and it is our hope that we have provided the reader with enough information to allow for full meditation on the Mother of the messiah's all-important role in salvation history. Allow us to introduce the reader to Daniel and the incredible wisdom of the Lord showered upon him. It was this very same prophet about whom some of the greatest Fathers of the Church wrote their most magnificent hymns[14], and it is this very same pillar of the faith who gives us the image of young virgins singing a hymn as humble before the Lord. Holy, humble, and full of love of God, we are at the doorsteps of the famed Magnificat. St. Jerome frequently noted how the first Christians were on the defensive from the moment they declared their undying love and loyalty to the messiah. These same Christians grew up memorizing many portions of Holy Writ from the most ancient and dustiest of manuscripts. We can imagine that an Ignatius of Antioch or a Clement of Alexandria would have been well aware of the words of the Virgin in her Magnificat: "My soul magnifies the Lord, and my spirit rejoices in God my Savior, for he has regarded the low estate of his handmaiden" (Lk 1:46–48).

The great Athanasius utilized Scripture to battle back the eponymous Ariomaniacs, making certain that with the strong foundation of the inerrant word and the pillar of the Church[15]serving as his very armor, he was able to provide a cogent defense of all things pertaining to the faith. It is here that we have utilized the primary principle of allowing the interpretation of Scripture by Scripture's very

---

[14] See for example, John Chrysostom, *Homily 5*, section 3, in *Saint Chrysostom: Homilies on the Acts of the Apostles and the Epistle to the Romans*, ed. P. Schaff, J. Walker, et al., trans. G. B. Stevens (New York: Christian Literature Company, 1889), 11:190-191.

[15]Athanasius, *Letter 2 to Serapion*, in *Works on the Spirit: Athanasius's Letters to Serapion on the Holy Spirit, and, Didymus's on the Holy Spirit*, trans. A. Radde-Gallwitz, and Lewis Ayres, Popular Patristics Series 43 (Yonkers NY: St Vladimir's Seminary Press, 2011), 108.

own sources! When we allow for the text to be brought to life within the very parameters and boundaries of its surrounding context and the sources to which it hearkens, we find that Mary calling Christ her Savior would not have been understood by the ancient Christians as ,thus, implying that she was indeed a sinner or was in a sinful state.

The fourth chapter of our study allows us to unveil the second chapter of St. Luke's Gospel account in a manner that is reminiscent of the "lovers of Christ." When we dusted off some of the oldest manuals on Mary, we noticed that our investigation would have to delve into Luke 2:22. For many years Christians seemed to squabble over the issue of Mary's purification in the Temple. Luke's purification account seemed to make things all the more confusing once an analysis of the Greek was undertaken. The purification in the Temple is clearly shown as being one that Jesus and Mary undergo *together*! But it must be asked: "What kind of purification is occurring?" Surely, a Christian would not believe that the sinless Christ had to undergo an actual cleansing for sin? Yet, the clear grammar utilized by Luke indicates that something different is occurring here. It is our great hope and desire that our in-depth analysis of the original text and our better understanding thereof, is no doubt laid out here in a concise manner. Here, we allow the reader to pull up a seat next to St. Luke and understand the clarity of his good news. It is also here where we provide you with an insight into how the early Church Fathers understood these key passages. In many cases, the Fathers would have been privy to the proper understanding of these passages by their access to apostolic traditions of interpretation. For example, St. Irenaeus noted that the great St. Polycarp was taught by the eyewitness, St. John the Theologian or Evangelist.[16] The Church Fathers were the recipients of the key by which we can understand Scripture. St. Cyril's Catechetical Lectures were clear that Scripture was a solid foundation, should people find themselves perplexed by a certain teaching. It was quite likely that allowing the text to interpret itself would unveil the answers to what seemed like a confusing issue. It is through this interpretive lens that we arrive at the Gospel of John and the Wedding at Cana. We hope that, rather than concluding the reader's continuing examination of the Virgin, we will have

---

[16] Irenaeus of Lyons, *Fragments from the Lost Writings of Irenaeus*, in *The Writings of Irenæus*, ed. A. Roberts & J. Donaldson, trans. A. Roberts and W. H. Rambaut (Edinburgh/London/Dublin: T. & T. Clark; Hamilton & Co.; John Robertson & Co, 1866), 2:159.

inspired you to open Scripture back up and look at it in a new manner. Perhaps now the present reader is able to grasp the importance of Mary and her role in the world of the great Evangelists. Modern Christians are frequently confounded at Christ's response to his Mother in the second chapter of John's account of the good news as they read the text in translation (or better through an interpretation). Was Jesus rebuking his Mother? After all, in verses 4 and 5 of chapter 2 he remarks: "And Jesus said to her, 'O woman, what have you to do with me? My hour has not yet come.' His mother said to the servants, 'Do whatever he tells you' " (John 2:4–5).

Many modern and contemporary scholars have noted possible ways that these texts seem to present a problem for Evangelicals and Catholics alike. If Christ was rebuking Mary, then why do Catholics, Orthodox, and even many Reformers insist on giving honor to the Virgin? The Evangelical conundrum comes in the commandment that one should honor their Mother and Father. Was Christ clearly violating one of the commandments, if he indeed responded in a harsh manner towards his own Mother? We will find that neither of these conclusions are viable. It is here that we peel back the layers of Holy Writ to present to you the true message that was being conveyed by the eyewitness, St. John. Mary's role in every account preserved by the holy Evangelists was an important one. The Virgin Mother pointed toward the holy mission of Jesus Christ, her messiah and savior. The consistency of Scripture is clear all-throughout. Mary is the perpetual virgin that embraced and vouchsafed the word with such love and devotion that she is rightly called all-holy and portrayed as a heroine for cause of Jesus Christ. [17]

---

[17] Modestus, *An Encomium on the Dormition of Our Most Holy Lady, Mary, Mother of God and Ever-Virgin*, in *On the Dormition of Mary: Early Patristic Homilies*, trans. Brian Daley, Popular Patristics Series 18 (Crestwood, NY: St Vladimir's Seminary Press, 1998), 84.

Chapter One:

Mary in the Gospel of Matthew and Mark

1.1 Who Are the Brothers and Sisters of Jesus?

Historical Christians and their Churches have often claimed to be Scriptural. Sometimes the savvy among them claim that there is a material or a formal sufficiency in Scripture for their doctrines. The "material sufficiency" claims that we can piece together newspaper clippings (like paper mâché) and construct an image of a New Testament doctrine formed out of these reworked passages glued together by reason. The "formal sufficiency" in Scripture means that either a very concrete or abstract doctrine is taught by a discernible and plain reading of the Bible text. Now, since distinctions of a philosophical nature are somewhat hard to come by in the New Testament, Bible-alone or *Sola-Scriptura* Christians sometimes walk away disappointed by others' mesmerizing amounts of theological distinctions with little to show for them when it comes to understanding a Biblical picture of Mary's life and vocation. The Bible, at first glance in the English language, seems to teach Jesus had a putative or adoptive dad (Joseph), a biological mom (Mary), and perhaps even biological siblings. There doesn't seem, at first glance, to be much to provide a fervent Bible reader to think differently. So, let us take a look at the Bible's evidence provided by Mark and Matthew that helps us get a handle on Jesus's family tree. Christians have a vested interest in knowing about Jesus's family; not only because he is their God, messiah, prophet, and hero, but because family lessons can often be taught to real Christians by applying Jesus's manner of relating to his own family for the benefit of Christians' daily lives in imitation of Jesus (the famous "What Would Jesus Do?"). So, we begin with a classically problematic passage that makes it hard to imagine Jesus as a spoiled, only child. We divide the story at the beginning of Mark chapter 6 into what is a so-called "chiasmus." Mark must have been a deli-worker according to scholars, because he loves making "Marcan sandwiches." Sometimes, Mark likes to begin a story (the top slice of bread), then jump to an aside story (the meat and cheese), and then return to finish his original story (the bottom slice of bread) and so make a so-called sandwich. Here, we have another of Mark's deli-delights: the layered cake. It's hardly millefoglie (a thousand-layered dessert), but it does get a little complex. We now take a look at the Gospel of Mark:

Chapter 6 [A₁] **¹ *Then he went out*** from there and came to *his own country* (*eis tên patrida autou*), *and his disciples followed Him.*

> **[B₁]** ² And when the Sabbath had come, he began **to teach** in the SYNAGOGUE. And many hearing him were astonished, saying, "Where did this man get these things? And what wisdom is this which is given to him, that *such mighty works* are performed **by his hands**! ³ Is this not the carpenter, the son of Mary, **[i.]** and **brother** (*adelphos*) of **James, Joses, Judas, and Simon**? **[ii.]** And are not his sisters (*adelphai*) here with us?" So they were offended at him.

[A₂] ⁴But Jesus said to them, "A prophet is not *without honor* except *in his own country* (*en têi patridi*),

> **[B₂]** among **[i.]** his own **relatives** (*en tois syngeneusin autou*),[18] and **[ii.]** [relatives] in his own house [of the father's family line from which one descends][19] (*en têi oikiai*)." ⁵ Now, *he could do no mighty work there*, except that **he laid His hands** on a few sick people and healed them. ⁶ And he marveled because of their unbelief.

[A₃] ***Then he went about*** *the villages in a circuit*, **teaching**.

Wow! Mark is a pretty organized storyteller! Notice, the story starts **[A₁]** with Jesus ***going out*** and **[A₃]** ends with ***him going out***. But this is not a happy tale, for Jesus goes **[A₁ and A₂]** *to his fatherland/homeland* as a prophet and is rejected in *his homeland* although a prophet. When preaching to them, the townsmen were **[B₁ verse 6]** marveling: Jesus had ordinary **[B₁ i.] relatives** who apparently don't live

---

[18] Mary is intentionally omitted by Jesus as someone allegedly dishonoring him according to his critics. She is exempted from the list of names by the enemies of Jesus but otherwise Jesus agrees with status of his other family members described in the list of Jesus's enemies.

[19] Henry Liddell, Robert Scott, and Henry Jones, *A Greek-English lexicon: With a revised supplement* (Oxford: Clarendon Press, 1996), v. *oikia*.

[**B₁ ii.**] within Jesus's family home ("here with us" [in Nazareth]) but these same cousins are lowborn so that they fail to single out [**B₁** verse 3] Jesus, son of Mary, as someone special in his youth. So, *how* could Jesus really be a prophet and [above verse 3] wise, like he sounds, with such [**B₁ i.**] no-name family members (let alone the female-cousin troublemakers)? Next, [**B₂**] Jesus was himself humanly astonished about [**B₁ i.**] his own extended family members choosing willfully and [verse 5] unwisely not to believe in him due to his uneventful earlier life, such that the Nazarene community members denied his wisdom and prophethood, though Jesus's lips resounded in their very ears. This is despite the Nazareth-community's admission that **his hands had cured the sick** such that their unbelief means that Jesus refused to reward them **by laying of hands** with the effect of doing miracles [**B₁** and **B₂**]. Notice, too, that the story goes from the broadest group of people related to Jesus to (in three steps) arriving at the closest group related to him: [**A₂**] Broadest: "fatherland/homeland," [**B₂ i.**] less broad: **kinsmen/brothers/cousins**, [**B₂ ii.**] least broad: kinsmen/sisters of his own household/family line. [**B₂**] Jesus **taught** unsuccessfully wisdom in his homeland, [**A₃**] but successfully **taught** it elsewhere; [**B₂ i.**] his **relatives** (not being children of the same mother, as must be the case according to proofs in the next paragraph,) caused him problems due to their lack of fame but [**B₂ ii.**] it was especially his own house or female relatives who are native dwellers in that locale who were actively responsible for others' unbelief (apparently, from Mark 3:20-21 [below], these extended family [or sisters] told people that Jesus was crazy!).

Let's now take a detailed look at Mark chapter 6, above, where there is a tit for tat for each thing mentioned! On the first like-hand, [**A₁ A₂ A₃**] each section of the story shares something in common, on the second like-hand sections [**B₁ B₂**] share other things or words in common, though there are also a few things exactly opposite one another: Now, let's look at the tit-for-tat in our layered [**B₁**] Marcan pastry: On the first like-hand, there are **James, Joses, Judas, and Simon**, and his sisters but, on the second-like hand, there are those whom Jesus designates both sisters and brothers according to his enemies' very same list, namely, those who are his own **relatives** (*syngeneusin*). Tit-for-tat [**B₁ B₂**]. Now, if we look up the most authoritative meaning of those who are mentioned by Jesus's villager-enemies in their list of people, [**B₂ i.**] Jesus summarily identifies his enemies' list of brethren as his **relatives**. He calls these effectively: "brothers and sisters of another mother."

This way of listing children of another mother, as one's sister is quite Biblical. For example, Abraham regarded his wife to be his very sister: "She is truly my sister, by my father, *not by my mother.*"[20] The Biblical scholar Jerome had long ago noticed this not only here, but also in Paul's use of the term "relatives" for his own blood kin.[21] If we look up Jesus's preferred term *syngenês* to identify his own designated brothers and sisters, we read in a lexicon/dictionary: "*syngenês: kinsfolk, kinsmen*; not properly applied to children (*ekgonoi*) in relation to their parents, and so opposite *ekgonoi* [...]"[22] So, for Jesus, who are these male brothers and female sisters? In answer, **[B₂ i.]** Jesus's own words identify them as "**his cousins**" (*tois syngeneusin*), that is, responding item-by-item to his enemies' list of people, as being his **kinsmen** or relatives from another mother![23]

Now, Jesus and his mom are clearly designated mother and son by Jesus' enemies. This Jewish identifying of a son by naming his *mother* ("son of Mary") is unusual in the Bible, as scholars note, since usually a son is mentioned in relation *to his father, unless the woman is a widow* (compare Luke 7:12).[24] All this means, then, is that Mary is a widow and mother of Jesus, but the others in Mark's list according to people in Nazareth are identified by Jesus as belonging to his **relatives** *who are not sons of his mother.* These **relatives**, especially his female

---

[20] Jerome, *Against Helvidius*, section 14, in *Jerome: Dogmatic and Polemic Works*, ed. Hirmigild Dressler, trans. John Hritzu, The Fathers of the Church 31 (Washington DC: Catholic University of America, 1981), 31.This suggests, too, that the first-century life of Mary or *Protevangelium of James* has a good Biblical basis for teaching that the children who are designated Jesus brothers and sisters are the sons of Joseph from a previous marriage.

[21] Jerome, *Against Helvidius*, section14.

[22] Liddell, Scott's and Jones, *Greek-English Dictionary*, v., *syngenês*.

[23] This matches exactly the familial division in Luke and Matthew. See section 1.2 below for Matthew's relevant familial divisions. Luke harmonizes with Jesus's meaning as follows: (1.) Mary's **female cousin** (*syngenis*) of another mother, Elizabeth (Luke 1:36), dwells (2.) in the house of Zachariah (*oikon Zachariou*) (Luke 1:40), but (3.) when she gives birth, Elizabeth's **cousins** (*oi syngeneis*) who live *outside* her husband's house hear at a distance about her birth and glorify God.

[24] See Brown, *Mary in the New Testament*, 64-65.

26

relatives in town, serve as too ordinary, even unimpressive people, in order to convince the rest of the town that Jesus really possesses wisdom and wonderworker capabilities based upon his family pedigree. Still, Jesus seems, per Mark's pastry-making, to make a distinction between his enemies' [B$_1$] specific appeal to his household in town versus Jesus's generic familial problems of his cousins' obscurity [B$_2$]. The problem of a lack of fame or importance includes for Jesus's enemies: (i.) Mary and (ii.) the rest of the family, but probably James, Joses, Jude and Simon are not the occasion for undermining Jesus, (iii.) for Jesus's remarks do not contradict his hometown unbelievers who are fixated especially on some negative reports or problems created by Jesus's female relatives or sisters.

While I consider the proof above to be pretty obvious and easily understandable for someone interested in Mark's artistry, vocabulary, style, and story-telling, I should also mention that **brother** (*adelphos*) can mean things like "**kinsman, relative**" in the Greek Old Testament, constantly quoted by Mark. For example, LXX Genesis 29:12 is where Jacob tells Rebecca: "that he is her father's **brother (kinsman**; *adelphos*)." Again, this happens in LXX Genesis 24:48: "the God of my master Abraham [...] led me by the right way to take the daughter of my master's **kinsman** (*adelphon*) for his son"; so that "**blood brother**" and "**kinsmen**" are the same.[25] It is also noteworthy, even important, as Rev. Dr. Laurentin has underlined, that the earliest Christian historian Hegessipus interpreted the Biblical reference to James, Brother of the Lord (Galatians 1:19; compare Acts 1:19), to mean: "first cousin" (*anepsios*) around AD 180.[26] Luke's Gospel justifies Mark (and Matthew below) as Synoptic or allied writers who use the same sources as Mark did. For Luke, Zachariah is a head of his household or extended family where Mary temporarily lives with Elizabeth her female **cousin** (*syngenis*; Luke 1:36). Jesus's plural-masculine preferred term "**cousins**" (*syngeneis*) is used for identification between Mary and Elizabeth and especially among unnamed other people who live outside of the household of Zachariah in his neighborhood; who hear the news of Elizabeth's giving birth (Luke 1:58). These **cousins** (*syngeneis*) explicitly live in different residences so that it takes a while for the rumors of Elizabeth's birth to get around. What is most intriguing,

---

[25] Jerome, *Against Helvidius*, section 14.

[26] René Laurentin, *Présence de Marie: Histoire, spiritualité, fondements doctrinaux* (Paris: Salvator, 2011), 32. See Eusebius, *Ecclesiastical History*,162 (book 3, chapter 12).

however, is that Luke uses the familial division in his infancy narrative when talking about Caesar's *census*! If we look at the vocabulary used by Mark, Luke, and Matthew (below), we immediately notice that all of them are aware of the technical familial divisions for the Israelite national census in LXX Numbers 1:2-3:

> Take a census of all the SYNAGOGUE/ASSEMBLY (*synagôgês*) of the sons of Israel, by their **clans/cousins** (*kata sygeneias autôn*), by their <u>patrilineal houses</u> (*kat'oikous patriôn autôn*), by number of name taken by their head (*kata kephalên autôn*), i.e., every male (*arsên*) twenty years old and above; everyone who can go out among the [armed] force of Israel.

The divisions are as follows: (1.) A patrilineal house (*oikos*) with heads (*kefalê*) above twenty years old, (2.) clansmen or cousins (*syngeneis*) who are blood relations broader than the patrilineal household, and (3.) the twelve tribes of Israel named according to Israel's son. These suggest that Hegessipus is correct and that James, Brother of the Lord, is probably a first cousin at best. Luke's designation of Mary as a "**female cousin**" *syngenis* is not only complementary to the divisions of Mark and Matthew (below), where "**cousin**" (*syngenis*) is said of Mary but explains why Elizabeth and John need not have been close to or very intimate with Mary prior or posterior to Elizabeth's conception; since they are neither immediate family, nor living near Mary's region. Finally, Luke ignored the better-known and current Roman familial divisions for the imperial census categories in preference to Mark (and Matthew), who speak Biblically by using the Mosaic Law's division of the family in Numbers. What is also interesting here, however, is that Luke's categories allow for Joseph to be a father or paterfamilias (*oikodespotês*) of his house wherein "extended family" live. Jesus's **cousins** (*syngeneis*) are either children of Joseph by a prior mother, other than Mary, or Jesus's **cousins** are his first cousins (the children of an aunt or uncle). This could mean (even if only one possibility among many) that Joseph was *neither* biological father of anyone in his extended household in Nazareth, of which he was the head, *nor* was Joseph hosting Mary's **cousins** (*syngeneis*) like **Joses** and **Simon** living in his household. Clearly, Luke describes Elizabeth's **cousins** (*syngeneis*) as people who live in entirely different residences like Elizabeth's neighbors (*paroikoi*). Altogether, we shall argue that evidence and parsimony suggest that Joseph's first wife more likely left him children, but it is possible that he had neither a first wife, nor children, once

28

all Biblical-familial vocabulary is systematized, as we logically show below, when treating Matthew's Gospel.

Returning to Jesus's female relatives who stayed in town and caused unbelief, we compare Mark 15:40-41: "Some women were watching from a distance. Among them were Mary Magdalene, **Mary the mother of James the younger and of Joseph**, and Salome. *In Galilee, these women had followed him and cared for his needs. Many other women who had come up with him to Jerusalem were also there*." There are many positively-mentioned women who, like Mary of Nazareth in Mark 3:31, followed Jesus around to minister to him and even go to Jerusalem with him (Mark 15:41). One can even get the sense that Mark mentions all the women named Mary (not to confuse his reader) to emphasize the rhetorical point made earlier by Jesus that –by following and ministering to Jesus ("doing God's will")– these women named Mary are *all his mothers*, since they "minister to him" and do God's will! On this score, I turn now to a last passage in Mark that is significant for understanding the problematic brothers and sisters of Jesus. Mark 3:31–34 recounts:

> Then Jesus' mother and **brothers** arrived. Standing outside, they sent someone in to call him. A crowd was sitting around him, and they told him, "Your mother and **brothers** are outside looking for you." "Who are my mother and **my brothers**?" he asked. Then he looked at those seated in a circle around him and said, "Here are my mother and **my brothers**! Whoever does God's will is **my brother and sister** and mother."

We think that Mark 6:1-6 is key to unravel the meaning of this passage for Mark as a writer. In chapter two, we will discuss Luke 11:27-28 that shows that Luke further develops his version of this passage as a major theme in his Gospel so that Mary is the first and only person up to the present time to fulfill perfectly Jesus's blessing: "Blessed are they who hear the word of God and keep it" (Luke 11:28). Mary, by repeating the angel Gabriel's "word" to her, which she "hears" at the annunciation, makes her subsequently declared "blessed" by the Spirit-inspired Elizabeth for "having believed." But Luke is Luke and Mark is Mark. Even so, if we are Bible-Christians, then we should see that, for Luke, Mary is the only person worthy of Jesus's blessing in Luke 11:28 "who hears the word of God and keeps it." As such, we are obliged to interpret Mark consistently with the clear message of Luke; namely, *if* Luke praises Mary by this phrase, then *so too must Mark be praising Mary by his similar phrase*! However, scholars do not like to anticipate conclusions in this way. They want the text of Scripture to speak for itself by interpreting the Bible through its own sources or the author's apparent intention. So, let us not *assume* that Mark must be like Luke and think Mary is blessed for that reason.

Even so, Mark 3:20-21 and 3:31-34 seem obviously to anticipate the big squabble and Jesus's family feud in Mark 6:1-6. First, we notice in Mark 3:20-21: "Then Jesus entered a house, and again a crowd gathered, so that he and his disciples were not even able to eat. When his family heard about this, they went to take charge of him, for they said, 'He is out of his mind.'" This is clearly a set of family members who is not actively following Jesus around, but they are aware of Jesus's ministry *only by hearing rumors* at home. Wouldn't you know it, this begins another millefoglie or layered pastry of Mark: [27]

[A₁] Mark 3:20-21: family "in his house"[28] (compare Mark 6:4) [i.] are those who think he is crazy

    [B₁] Mark 3:22: Jesus is accused of having a demon!

        [C.] Mark 3:23-29: Jesus's refutation of the accusation of being possessed

        by appealing to a family household divided against itself

    [B₂] Mark 3:30: Jesus is accused of having a demon [again]!

[A₂] Mark 3:31-32: Mother, **brothers and sisters/kinsmen** (compare Mark 6:3) come.

---

[27] I agree, overall, with the structure summarized by Brown, *Mary in the New Testament*, 54.

[28] Compare LXX Numbers 1:2. See Phillip Budd, *The Word Bible Commentary: Numbers* (Waco TX: Word Biblical Commentaries, 1984), 5:1-2.

[i.] Q: Who are these mother and **brothers and sisters**? **[ii.]** A: Doers of God's will

Notice, unlike his extended-family dwelling in his <u>home</u> *who do not follow him around* (identified as his female relatives/sisters in Mark 6:4), Jesus's mother and **kinsmen** are mentioned a second time. The kinswomen again are distinguished from his lowborn but faithful **relatives** who follow him around and minister to him along with Jesus's mother. Jesus's mother and **relatives** in Mark 3:31-34 are following him around but neither are they causing trouble, nor rejecting him like those (Mark 3:20-21; 6:3) who live in his family <u>home</u> of Jesus's patrilineal descent.

We now compare Mark's source for his division of Jesus's family to the Septuagint: "Receive the beginning of the GATHERING/SYNAGOGUE of the [biological] sons of Israel (*hiôn Israêl*), by their **relatives/brothers** (*kata syngeneias*), by the <u>houses</u> derived from their fathers' [line] (*kat'oikous patriôn autôn*) by number; every male by name under the [male] head [in the family]." The enemies of Jesus are simply using a Biblical division of Jesus's family by sons of Jesus's mother Mary (=Jesus), then by naming **relatives** (not of the same father), and those in the patrilineal <u>house</u> (compare Luke 2:5: "he [Joseph] was from the <u>house</u> [*oikou*] and patrilineal descent (*patrias*) of David).[29] The original groupings would have been in Hebrew: larger "**clans**," smaller "fathers' houses," and a male-adult head (of a family or a bachelor fit for military service). The term: Father's houses, means precisely "extended family." Notice, that what is missing from Jesus's enemies' list and from Jesus himself is any reference to a family "by [male] head." This suggests that neither the enemies of Jesus in Mark 6:1-6, nor Jesus, think that Joseph, his (putative) father, is any longer the living head of the household and of his own offspring who are probably his daughters living there!

Yet another proof of our interpretation of Mark 3:20-32 is found in a wordplay used by Mark to distinguish the <u>stay-at-home</u> cousins from Jesus's mother and faithful-lowborn **relatives**; namely, Mark 3:20: "He [Jesus] *comes* (*erchetai*) to the house and the crowd *comes* with (*synerchetai*) him" and "his mother and his brethren *come* (*erchontai*)" (Mark 3:31). Jesus is a guy who "comes" and a good-believing crowd "comes" and Mary along with her **relatives**

---

[29] See also Jerome, *Against Helvidius*, 14.

"come." So, those who "come" are the good guys.[30] Who are indisputably the bad guys? Well, Mark writes about those who "come out (*eksêlthon*)" calling him "*out* of his mind (*eksesti*)" (Mark 3:21). Clearly there is the "in-crowd" ("coming") and there is the "*out*-crowd" ("coming *out*"). Mary and **her relatives** imitate the "in-crowd," but the patrilineal house is coming "*out*" to call Jesus "*out* of his mind." Mary and the relatives are objectively good guys for Mark, for they are coming from the right direction![31]

Jesus is able to do miracles with those who accompany him on his ministry. So, are Jesus's mother and **relatives** *doing God's will by following him wherever he goes* or are they like his female relatives in his hometown who don't follow him and are the very scandal by which his townsmen reject him as a prophet? So, what is the point here? The answer is in Mark 15:41: "The women [two Marys and many other women, one of whom is probably including the mother of Jesus's **relatives**], when he was in Galilee, were following (*êkolouthoun*) him and ministering to him." The point is that the mother and **cousins** are honorable, insofar as they are the ones clearly serving or ministering to Jesus and, therefore, do Jesus's will. Anyone listening to Jesus's talk in Mark chapter 3 and who follows afterwards God's will can be Jesus's mother and **relative**. Jesus does mention in Mark chapter 6 that his fatherland provides him –being a prophet– with no honor, for his **cousins** in that fatherland have no particular honors, and especially those in his direct bloodline of descent at his home are completely dishonorable, but Jesus excludes from his list of dishonor his own mother, though Jesus's enemies clearly implicate Mary as a non-entity *not* contributing to his prophetic reputation in their

---

[30] Unfortunately, Brown, *Mary in the New Testament*, 11, writes: "There are indications that Mary did not follow Jesus about during the ministry but remained at home with the family" He notes (ibid.): "In Mark 3:31 [...] Mary *comes* with Jesus' brothers to where Jesus is, and Mark 3:21 implies that they had set out from another place on this journey." But Brown fails to note the precision of Mark, Jesus is "coming" and the crowd is "coming with" while Mary and the brothers, like Jesus, "come" but the family at Jesus's house "come out." There are three groups: (1.) The Jesus crowd, (2.) the Mary and cousins crowd not with the Jesus crowd, and (3.) the stay-at-home but "coming out" crowd.

[31] My analysis counters Brown, *Mary in the New Testament*, 55-56, who fails to notice the family divisions according to LXX Numbers 1:2 and the wordplays.

list at Mark 6:3.[32] Shouldn't Jesus repeat, too, in Mark 6:3-4 that his mother, just like his cousins, provide him with no positive honor? He doesn't do that! What we should infer from that seems to be that Mary represents a case that Jesus does not see as detracting from his honor as a prophet, but Mark clearly avoids mentioning to his reader anything –from her honorable lineage to Mary's virgin birth– in order for us to have a clear idea when reading Mark in isolation why Mark exempts Mary from Jesus's naughty list of people detracting from his extrinsic honor as a prophet.[33] What we do know in Mark is that relatives who stay <u>home</u> (who don't follow him) are not true family; this is not his mother or relatives who go around with him, who are by Jesus's own words, his true family. The implications are grave for Mark 6:1-6: Jesus's physical or biological-female extended family are – to him– not truly his family, for they did not do the will of God. He could not heal the locals since a condition for such was believing in him and following him. Therefore, he had to **teach** God's will, wisdom, and show miracles in other towns having nothing to do with Jesus's patrilineal bloodline!

Conclusions

Jesus responded to a list of names by his enemies. Jesus clearly identifies those in his <u>house(hold)</u> (*oikos*; *oikia*) and his brothers and sisters as his own "**kinsmen** (*syngeneis*)." Jesus, thereby, definitively excludes the list of brethren and <u>household</u> people in Mark 3:31-32 and the formal list of **names, brethren,** and sisters in Mark 6:3 from being biological sons or children (*ekgonos, -oi*) of Mary.[34] Jesus also refuses to name Mary in accord with his enemies' list, for reasons that Mark does not give. After all, Jesus is okay with repeating his enemies list about other family members who dishonor Jesus, but Mary is somebody apparently *not* mentioned by Jesus through disagreement with his enemies, with the result that she must not bring him obscurity or disgrace according to Mark 6:3.

---

[32] Brown, *Mary in the New Testament*, 63, fails to consider that Jesus's striking of Mary off his enemies list is a kind of honor in itself.

[33] Some scholars suggest that Mark is aware of the virgin birth narrative or material here, but the evidence is not clear. See Brown, *Mary in the New Testament*, 61-63.

[34] My conclusions are the opposite of Brown, *Mary in the New Testament*, 72.

Additionally, we can infer several other things about Mary throughout the rest of our book: (1.) Mark's early Gospel (material prior to AD 70) tries to avoid Mary, mother of Jesus, as a focal point;[35] (2.) This will change after the extended-family monopoly that was taken up by Jesus's blood relatives to seize power in some churches in greater Palestine is broken during the Jewish war (ending in AD 70);[36] (3.) After nepotism is thwarted in the early church, in harmony with the earliest Church historian Hegessipus reporting on Jesus's kinsmen as head of the Jerusalem church (writing around AD 180), later Gospel writers (Matthew, Luke and John) feel more comfortable making more deliberate inclusions of Mary in the Gospel texts since a greater mention of the influence and goodness of Jesus's relatives will not risk emboldening Jesus's-relatives' party in Palestine. See Mark 3:21, where bad behavior and unbelief of Jesus's extended family members serve to support the Evangelists' church over Jesus's-relatives' attempt at a genetically lead church; (4.) The result is that Mary's *familial* contribution to Jesus's ministry (as well as other relatives) becomes less politicized and more of an historical and theological question of interest for Christian readers; (5.) In the end, since the Evangelists are, to a greater or lesser extent, all using some of the same basic reports and stories about Jesus, they all make sure to include the anti-relatives

---

[35] With respect to Mary's role at the Resurrection, see the patristic tradition known to John the Geometer (born AD 934/5-died AD 1000), *The Life of the Virgin: Translated with an Introduction and Notes* (New Haven: Yale University Press, 2012), 119-120, which reflects ancient beliefs about Mary's omission saving the Gospel from nepotism: "Even though the Evangelists mention none of this in the account of the Resurrection it is for this reason that they left of the mother's witness to preclude any doubt and show that no one would it as reason for unbelief; that the vision of the resurrection was reported by the mother." For true authorship (not Ps.-Maximus the Confessor [!] according to Shoemaker) of this work, see Nicholas Constas, "The Story of an Edition: Antoine Wenger and John Geometres' *Life of the Virgin Mary*," in *Marian Narratives in Texts and Images*, ed. Thomas Arentzen and Mary Cunningham (Cambridge: Cambridge University Press, 2019), 22.

[36] First see Eusebius Eusebius Pamphili, *Ecclesiastical History: Book 1-5*, trans. Roy Deferrari, The Fathers of the Church: A New Translation (Washington DC: The Catholic University of America Press, 1965), 63-64 (book 1, chapter 7), for the history of Jesus's extended family propagandizing their blood relation to Jesus. For evidence of Jesus's family and power in the first-century church, see Chris Maunder, "Mary and the Gospel Narratives," in *The Oxford Handbook of Mary*, ed. Chris Maunder (Oxford: Oxford University Press, 2019), 23-25.

stories (to a varying degree) in their Gospels since memories of the nepotism and attempted hostile takeover by "*la famiglia*" (*mafiosi*[!]) of the church are fresh enough in people's minds that it never hurts in Luke (11:27) and John (7:5) to occasionally remind Christians that Jesus's extended family members are sometimes a detriment to the church, sometimes a help, even if there is a far more negative image of them in Mark's Gospel due to the ongoing battle for control between Jesus's mainly non-familial appointed successors and those who are known in the Gospels', Hegessipus's, and Eusebius's (around 300 AD) histories; namely, family members who tried to ride on the coattails of Jesus's fame in order to wield power, influence, and gain from the first-century church.[37]

Mark's Gospel, then, avoids mentioning the virgin conception, the virgin birth, and much of Mary's role in the history of salvation. This was strategically necessary to emphasize the universal (versus privately familial) nature of the Church and salvation. As the church began to be more integrated between relatives and non-relatives of Jesus, and as early-church leaders increasingly were taken from people not of Jesus's bloodline, the risk of promoting Mary and other cousins' contributions to the early Church was lessened. Hence, the later Evangelists included an increasing amount of material about the virtuous and celebratory relatives of Jesus; still not without some reminders of how petty Jesus's cousins and extended family could be. Finally, culminating in Luke and John, mention of Mary (the infancy narratives and John the Evangelist's Mary at the cross) seems to pose very little risk of being used for propaganda by Jesus's extended family; probably because (sadly) many of them were killed, exiled, enslaved, or dispossessed of their wealth in the Jewish war. The result is: the more that Jesus's apostles and their hand-picked successors became the universally recognized leaders of the Church, the more Mary could be given a place of honor without risk; this is most evident in her privileged place in the midst of the Apostles at Pentecost (Acts 2:1-4) in the upper room, omitted by Gospels for the reasons just mentioned. Since we can now see that Luke 11:27-28, John 2:4, and even Mark 6:1-6 can all be calmly and consistently explained by the principles of: Interpreting Scripture by its sources and by fellow-Scripture, Reading the New Testament literally, and finding harmony in the Gospels, we finally conclude that the position

---

[37] Eusebius *Ecclesiastical History,* 59-65 (book 1, chapter 7, paragraphs 11–14). The more positive aspects of the familial narrative are also related in ibid., 161-162 (book 3, chapter 11).

and role of Mary is correctly highlighted and celebrated by each Evangelist according to the needs and inspiration that was proper for the time and place of any one Gospel. We shall see that Mary shall be confirmed not only as a doer of God's will (according to Mark), along with her cousins, but she will be individually affirmed as: Ark of the Covenant (Luke 1), the New Daughter of Jephthah (Luke 1), The New Abraham and Sarah (Luke 1), The New Hannah (Luke 1), The New Mother of Samson (Matthew 1-2, Luke 1), the hearer and keeper of God's will and word (Mark 6; Luke 11), and The New Widow of Elijah (John 2). To be Biblical, then, is to concede to Mary the honor bestowed by each of these characterizations because they point toward and complement the saving ministry of her son who is God, messiah, and savior.

1.2 The Virgin Birth and Perpetual Virginity in Matthew Chapter 1

Jesus naturally has some pretty good reasons for holding Joseph, Mary, and his **brethren** or **relatives** in honor in Matthew's and Mark's Gospels. Matthew sets up the reader's preview of the evidence for Jesus to exclude his honorable and putative father Joseph and his honorable mother Mary (not to mention his **four male cousins**) from the disreputable women of the <u>household</u> among his extended family mentioned in Mark 3:20-21, 30-31 and Mark 6:1-6. We find out, from Matthew chapters 1-2, that Jesus's reasons for honoring his parents must include both the virgin birth and Joseph's role in protecting Mary's honor during and after that event. So, we immediately turn to Matthew 1:1-22, essentially asserting that the divine seed or offspring (from the Spirit) in Mary's womb is said to be "in her." This is meant to say that she did not biologically undergo parthenogenesis by nature but that the Spirit miraculously produced what was found to be in her without need of her own, or of her putative husband's, biological cooperation. In the end, Mary was the unique human contributor of flesh or genetic material for the Spirit's use in Matthew's Gospel.

Now, we see in Matthew 1:19 that "Joseph her husband was a just man." Interestingly, however, he is also called honorably: "o son of David" (Matthew 1:20). He's already saddled with a double honor, first by Matthew's opinion of him and then by an angel's designation of him as an heir of David. This prominent position is followed up immediately by telling Joseph that Mary's virginal (LXX Isaiah 7:14) conception was predicted by a prophet. This looks suspiciously like Matthew is setting up his reader to know that Jesus's enemies (later, below, in

Matthew 13:55) are simply wrong by dishonoring Joseph and Mary, for –while Joseph is a just heir to the promise of David– Mary's pregnancy is the fulfilment of the prophet Isaiah's (7:14) prediction. So, how can it be that Joseph and Mary of Nazareth do not bestow honor to Jesus in his fatherland where they live when Joseph is described as just and Davidic, while Mary is the direct object of the saving prophecy of Israel? Quite to the contrary, Joseph and Mary are left excluded from Jesus's his blood relatives in his reply to his enemies' detailed blacklist in Matthew chapter 13 (just like Mark 6:1-6 above). Jesus omits Joseph and Mary from the blacklist precisely because his parents are already advertised as honorable to the reader in the first two chapters of Matthew. We shall see that only Joseph's children (most likely) from his first marriage leave Jesus without honor in Matthew's Gospel; but these are specifically his relatives who dwell in Joseph's house at Nazareth at a time when Joseph is presumably dead.

Among scholars, even if they dispute other passages on the virgin birth, Matthew's Gospel indisputably defends and promotes Mary as someone conceiving and giving birth in virginity, for the angel tells Joseph that Mary has miraculously conceived directly from the Holy Spirit (Matthew 1:21). This event is merely a confirmation of the oldest witness to Isaiah (7:14) in the Greek Old Testament predicting that one day the line of David will know a wonder-child called God-with-us, who will be born of a virgin (*parthenos*) (Matthew 1:23). Joseph, sometime after the angel's announcement, "took Mary as his official wife (*gynaika*), all the while being unaccustomed to know her, until the time when she gave birth and named him Jesus" (Matthew 1:26).

What is interesting here is that Joseph "was unaccustomed to know her" or "not used to knowing her" or "was not knowing her." Unlike all Old Testament usages of the euphemism "to know," Matthew chose to render it in the indicative imperfect or continuous action in the past whose effect is felt in the present. Oppositely, in LXX Genesis 4:1 it reads: "Adam knew Eve his wife and she, upon coming together with him, conceived Cain (*egnô Euan tên gynaika autou kai syllabousa eteken ton Kain*)"; this is the same for Seth (LXX Genesis 4:24). The exact same phrase is used for Cain conceiving with his wife (LXX 4:16). We find the pithier version of this phrase used by Matthew only in (LXX=) 1 Samuel 1:19, where it says that a husband "knew Hannah his wife (*egnô tên Anan gynaika autou*)." Other grammatical forms, such as participles for "knowing (sexually)," are also typically in a past or perfect form, neither in the present, nor imperfect, when referring to "having sex (knowing)" or "not having sex (not knowing)" with regard to a woman or to man. Matthew (and Luke 1:34) uniquely attested that Joseph was continuously unused to any sexual intimacy with Mary. However, a good question arises among both ancient and contemporary Christians, for the verse reads in isolation: "He was unaccustomed to know her, until the time when she gave birth." In Greek, this "until" has the same ambiguity as in English. "Until" means in the Bible: "up to that time and beyond" but also: "up to that time and not beyond." So it is ambiguous. Instead of reinventing the wheel, we present St. John Chrysostom who explains how the Greek speakers of his day understand the use of the preposition "until":

> And when Joseph had taken her, "he had no relations with her until she had borne a son." Matthew has here used the word "until" not that you should suspect that afterward Joseph did know her but to inform you that before the birth the Virgin was wholly untouched by man. But why then, it may be said, has he used the word "until"? Because it is common in Scripture that this expression is used without reference to specific, limited times. Here are three examples. First, in the narrative of the ark it was said that "the raven did not return *until* the earth was dried up," yet the raven did not return even after that limited time. Second, when discussing God the Scripture says, "You are from everlasting to everlasting,"[42] but there is no implication here that some limit is being fixed—rather the opposite. Third, when preaching the gospel beforehand and saying, "In his days may righteousness flourish, and peace abound, until the moon be no more!" it is not thereby setting a temporal limit to this beautiful part of creation. So then here likewise, it uses the word "until" to make certain what was before the birth, but as to what follows, it leaves some further inference to be made. So it is necessary to learn what Matthew teaches: that the Virgin was untouched by man until the birth. But the rest is left for you to perceive, both as a consequence of the previous narrative and what was later acknowledged: that not even after having become a mother and having been counted worthy of a new sort of travail and a childbearing so strange, could

that righteous man ever have permitted himself to have sexual relations with her.[38]

Additionally, we have the expert testimony of St. Jerome:

> And when Joseph had taken her, "he had no relations with her until she had borne a son." Matthew has here used the word until not that you should suspect that afterward Joseph did know her but to inform you that before the birth the Virgin was wholly untouched by man. But why then, it may be said, has he used the word until? Because it is common in Scripture that this expression is used without reference to specific, limited times. Here are three examples. First, in the narrative of the ark it was said that "the raven did not return until the earth was dried up," yet the raven did not return even after that limited time. Second, when discussing God the Scripture says, "You are from everlasting to everlasting," but there is no implication here that some limit is being fixed— rather the opposite. Third, when preaching the gospel beforehand and saying, "In his days may righteousness flourish, and peace abound, until the moon be no more!" it is not thereby setting a temporal limit to this beautiful part of creation. So then here likewise, it uses the word until to make certain what was before the birth, but as to what follows, it leaves some further inference to be made. So it is necessary to learn what Matthew teaches: that the Virgin was untouched by man until the birth. But the rest is left for you to perceive, both as a consequence of the previous narrative and what was later acknowledged: that not even after having become a mother and having been counted worthy of a new sort of travail and a childbearing so strange, could that righteous man ever have permitted himself to have sexual relations with her.

Elsewhere, he continues:

> Helvidius [who rejects Mary's perpetual virginity] is at much superfluous trouble to make this word "know" refer to carnal knowledge rather than to acquaintance, as though any had ever denied that; or as if the follies to which he replies had ever

---

[38] John Chrysostom, *Homily on the Gospel of Matthew*, 5.3.

occurred to any person of common understanding. He then goes on to say, that the adverb "until" denotes a fixed time when that should take place, which had not taken place before; so that here from the words, "He knew her not until she had brought forth her first-born Son," it is clear, he says, that after that he did know her. And in proof of this he heaps together many instances from Scripture. To all this we answer, that the word "until" is to be understood in two senses in Scripture. And concerning the expression, "knew her not," he has himself shewn, that it must be referred to carnal knowledge, none doubting that it is often used of acquaintance, as in that, "The child Jesus tarried behind in Jerusalem, and His parents knew not of it." (Luke 2:43) In like manner "until" often denotes in Scripture, as he has shewn, a fixed period, but often also an infinite time, as in that, "Even to your old age I am He" (Isaiah 46:4). Will God then cease to be when they are grown old? Also the Savior in the Gospel, "Lo, I am with you always, even to the end of this world" (Matthew 28:20). Will He then leave His disciples at the end of the world? Again, the Apostle says, "He must reign till He has put His enemies under His feet" (1 Corinthians 15:25). Be it understood then, that that which if it had not been written might have been doubted of, is expressly declared to us; other things are left to our own understanding. So here the Evangelist informs us, in that wherein there might have been room for error, that she was not known by her husband until the birth of her Son, that we might thence infer that much less was she known afterwards.[39]

The main value of these saintly and scholarly arguments lies in the fact that a verb in the indicative (whether present or past), along with the word "until" (*heôs*), need not express limiting and changing a situation, but it may express ambiguously either a limit, or (conversely) no limit. While this is true, Helvidius and anonymous naysayers (known to St. John Chrysostom) lacked knowledge that moderns have to reinforce Helvidius's argument. After perusing all cases of "until the time when" (*heôs hou*) in the Septuagint, I was nearly led to believe, as some scholars state, that no example exists where a verb in the indicative imperfect + "until" ever signifies an action to continue following the preposition "until." For example: "The

---

[39] Jerome, *Against Helvidius*, section 5.

boy *was sitting until* the school bell rang." They claim that we never find this in the Old Testament or New Testament meaning that the boy *continues to sit after the bell*. In reality, the infancy narrative in the Gospel Luke is a perfect instance of the imperfect + "until" signaling a continuation of the activity of the verb proceeding "until." Let us take a look: "The child was growing and was empowered by the Spirit and he was (*ên*) in the desert places until (*heôs*) the day of his manifestation to Israel" (Luke 1:80). John continuously lived in desert places. We have no reason to believe that he moved his house after he became famous. So, while Chrysostom's and Jerome's correct examples *do not explicitly include* an imperfect indicative verb + "until," they actually do know these intricacies of Greek grammar; when an aorist active verb and other indicative verbs are used in the New Testament and they are followed by "until the time (when she gave birth)" the action of the verb can continue. However, the definitive solution lies in a detailed analysis of the literary structure of Matthew 1:1-18:

[A₁] A book of *generation* of **Jesus**, **Messiah**, Son of David Son of God (Matthew 1:1)

> [B₁] Abraham generated Isaac–Jesse generated David the King

> [C₁] David generated Solomon from the [wife of] Uriah–Josiah generated Jeconiah and his brothers at the time of the exile to Babylon.

> [D₁] After the exile to Babylon: Jeconiah generated Shealtiel–Jacob generated Joseph the husband of Mary [his wife] from whom

[A₂] *was generated* **Jesus** who is called **Messiah** (Matthew 1:16)

> [B₂] "**from** (*apo*) Abraham **until** (*heôs*) David" = 14 generations, and

> [C₂] "**from** (*apo*) David **until** (*heôs*) the exile of Babylon" = 14 generations, and

> [D₂] "**from** (*apo*) exile **until** (*heôs*) the Messiah" = 14 generations

[A₃] *The generation* of **Jesus**, **Messiah** was as follows (Matthew 1:18)

> [D₃] Joseph did (*epoiêsen*) [as told] "**from** (*apo*) a dream" [...] and took to himself his wife (*parelaben tên gynaika autou*,)[25] –even while

41

accustomed not to know her– **until** the time when she bore a son (*kai ouk eginôsken autên, heôs hou eteken hion*)."

Wow! Matthew is just as complex a storyteller as Mark was. Notice the clear patterns. For our purposes the pattern that betrays the meaning of **until** occurs in [B₂-D₂]: There is a time or source "**from** which" that encapsulates all the generations enumerated into groups of fourteen **until** the last member in a series of physical or biological productions is named at the end of an historical grouping. Then, there begins something brand new. Notice that the dramatically new items are: [B₂] **From** Abraham **until** a new kingdom, [C₂] **From** anew kingdom **until** a defeat and exile, and [D₂] **From** an exile **until** a new anointed or "Son of David," or a new kingdom. So, what should we expect with [D₃]? We should expect *a first generated* child for a new kingdom in a series until *a last generated* child of that kingdom in the very same series! Of course, this makes us immediately realize that Jesus is the only child in his series, or rather the lack of any series of children! His generation begins at his annunciation (by an angel) and his line ends with himself (when he dies, he has no wife, *generation*, or siblings). That is what this list implies. Still, even if the **from-until** [D₃] makes it obvious that Jesus is the end term of his family lineage in [A₃], what sense can we make of "**until**"?

In answer, notice my **bold commas** in a complex or compound sentence with three verbs [D₃]: "He *did*, and he *took*, even while he *was knowing* not, until [...]."Matthew expects his reader to link all three verbs falling in between his **from-until** markers in order to understand the *generation* of Jesus. That means all three verbs must be considered as part of the compound sentence from his word: "**after**," up to his other marker: "**until**." This construction means that the sentence should read: "He took her as if his wife even though he wasn't having sex with her." Why is this reformulation significant? Well, it means that the principal verbs are: He did + he took (in the aorist), which is an aorist construction + "**until**" as the primary verb for the sentence. Finally, we can justify St. John and St. Jerome. The clause to which "until the time when she bore" should be attached is "he took her as his wife." This means more completely: "and he took her as (if) his wife**,** **until** she gave birth**,** even while he was having no sex with her." Notice, "**until**" has the same meaning as Matthew 28:12: "I will be with you **until** the end of the world." After all, Joseph did not throw Mary out of his house after she gave birth. Instead, he housed her, then she gave birth, and next he continued to house her,

42

even while having continuously no sex with her. In fact, after independently arriving at this conclusion, we were pleased to see that Chrysostom knew this exact reading. Notice with St John Chrysostom our very same punctuation –as interpreted by some modern editors– that separates "he knew her not" from "until she had brought forth [...]" by a **comma**, so that "**until**" can be properly adjoined to: "he had taken her (into his house) [...]":

> "And took unto him Mary his wife." See thou how continually the evangelist uses this word, not willing that that mystery should be disclosed as yet, and annihilating that evil suspicion? "And when he had taken her, he knew her not, **until** she had brought forth her first-born Son (*paralabôn de autên, ouk eginôsken autên, heôs hou eteke ton hion autês prôtotokon*)." He hath here used the word "**until**," not that thou shouldest suspect that afterwards he did know her, but to inform thee that before the birth the Virgin was wholly untouched by man. But why then, it may be said, hath he used the word, "until"? Because it is usual in Scripture often to do this, and to use this expression without reference to limited times. For so with respect to the ark likewise, it is said, "The raven returned not till the earth was dried up."[40]

Chrysostom's reinterpretation of the reading is exactly what we have done and supposes that the Matthew 1:24-25 contains an aorist "he had taken" (*parelaben* = *paralabôn*) + "**until**" construction. Hence, the phrase: "while he was not knowing her" –similar to the "**until**" phrase– is a dependent clause on the main clause: "He had taken her." Chrysostom is one of several marvelously ancient witnesses to the correct reading or interpretation of the text.[41]

---

[40] John Chrysostom, *Homily on the Gospel of Matthew*, 5.5.

[41] I have checked ancient manuscripts such as the *codex Alexandrinus* but Greek manuscripts are typically devoid of punctuation to betray how Antique and Late Antique Christians read the text. In rare cases, when there is punctuation in manuscripts, whether Greek or Latin, I find what in English punctuation is a colon or ":" exclusively here: "*ouk eginôsken autên: heôs hou eteke* [...]". Editors agreeing with our punctuation by interpretation of commentaries or citations of this passage include: Jerome, *Adversus Helvidium de Mariae virginitate perpetua* (Patrologia Latina 23, cols. 193-216); Epiphanius Latinus, *Interpretatio Evangeliorum*, ed. A. Erickson, Corpus Patrum

Another reason why Chrysostom's reading –between the two possible readings discussed– must be the correct construction relies on Mary's child being the beginning and end term of an entire line of *generation* from Matthew's (1:17-18) **from-to** paradigm: Whenever there is a mother listed, she is described with each and every one of her known children according to the paradigm in Matthew 1:3, 5-6, 16. Each woman named in Matthew's list had the exactly limited number of children explicitly named as her own! Let us take a look:

Judah bore two children, Perez and Zerah, from the wife Tamar (Matthew 1:3)
Salmon bore the total of one child from the wife Rahab (Matthew 1:5)
Obed bore the total of one child from the wife Ruth (Matthew 1:5)
David bore only one living child, Solomon, from the wife of another man Uriah (Matthew 1:6)
From the Holy Spirit came the offspring Jesus who is from the wife Mary (1:16, 18)

The only constant in this pattern is clear: Matthew emphasizes that Jesus was an only son by picking women in the Old Testament and by listing completely their known children. When Mary is mentioned, the only adjustment that is made is to replace Jesus's lacking paternity (due to the virgin birth [!]) with the action of the Holy Spirit. But Mary's womb –like the other women – is implied to bear only the child/ren that Matthew explicitly named; who is Jesus alone for Mary. This means that she was a virgin before Joseph took her in, and Joseph took her in **until** (and even after) she gave birth, but all the while (before and after) had no relations with her. Therefore, she was a perpetual virgin. It can also plausibly mean: Joseph took her into his house (patrilineal house in Bethlehem, as a son of David), **until** she gave birth, and then Joseph left with Mary and the child (to Egypt[?] or to Nazareth[?]), although never having relations with her.

Latinorum 914 (Turnhout: Brepols, 1933), 4; Anonymous (c. 9th century), *In Matthaeum*, ed. Bengt Löfstedt, Corpus Christianorum: Continuatio Mediaevalis 159 (Turhout: Brepols, 2003), 5.

As we shall see in our elongated discussion in chapter 2 on Luke 1:34, the use of the indicative ("I do not know" and here "he was not knowing") is exactly the same for Mary in Luke 1:34. In other words, both the Evangelists Matthew and Luke used a non-perfective form of "to know" to mean "to keep having sex" such that "*not* to know" means to keep *not* having intercourse. This phraseology is unique to Matthew and Luke and may betray a common, if peculiar, reading between them (LXX Judges 11:39) for conceptualizing perpetual refrain from sex. What is surprising, however, is that it also creates a dilemma: If the meaning of Mary's "I do not know man" (read in light of LXX Judges 11:39) means: "I am vowed always not to have relations with a man," then Joseph's designation: "He was not knowing her," could imply that "he was vowed to virginity and therefore never knew her." This is shocking and puzzling. How do we account for Jesus's brothers and sisters, if they are not the children of Joseph's first marriage? It is a problem but since brothers and sisters may designate first cousins, it is possible that Joseph has no biological children in his household. This would fit the normal annunciation patterns where both husband and wife are childless prior to the miracle of conception. It is tempting to develop Joseph's perpetual virginity from Matthew's passage in isolation, but Mark's Gospel and what remains for us to investigate in Matthew make it more likely by virtue of parsimony that Joseph had had another wife prior to Mary. While Joseph too could have been a virgin, such a reading is somewhat more difficult by complexity (not by contradiction) in light of how the brothers and sisters of Jesus are associated with the house of Joseph in Nazareth. It is also difficult because Luke chapter 1 underlines that Mary was a virgin explicitly "who knows not man" by quoting the perpetual virginity passage uniquely in Judges 11:39, while Joseph is never identified as a virgin beforehand who was"not continuously knowing her."[42] This can only argue to commit Joseph explicitly to perpetual continence after his marriage to Mary. All the same, this phrase unequivocally means that as long as he was married to Mary, he had no relations with her. Now Jesus, according to Mark 6:4, is most probably identifying

---

[42] See *[Protoevangelium =] The Infancy Gospel of James*, 9.8, in *The Infancy Gospel of James and Thomas*, trans. and ed. Robert Hock, The Scholars Bible 2 (Santa Rosa CA: Polebrock, 1995), chapter 9.11-12, where Joseph – the moment he takes Mary from the temple – he leaves her alone and sequestered at his physical domicile. He refuses to dwell physically with her at home because he is a carpenter and is in the midst of building several houses. Chapter 9 of the work sets up and repeats again and again the point that Joseph took her only to protect and sequester her –not wanting to marry her– and to preserve her virginity prior to birth.

his brothers and sisters as cousins who are children of another mother (but not necessarily of another father) but it is ultimately for the reader to decide whether the second possibility of Jesus's brothers and household should be thought of as merely first cousins of Joseph.[43]

1.3 The Brothers and Sisters of Jesus in Matthew Chapter 1

While it cannot be doubted that Mary bore *only* one child listed by Matthew, just like the paradigms Matthew provides with each and every mother in his list of Jesus's ancestors, so does Matthew use his opening chapter to argue for the virginal conception, virgin birth, and perpetual virginity of Mary. But Matthew additionally prepares his readers to anticipate the complex family structure in Jesus's household in Nazareth (Matthew 13:51-58). In order to prepare Matthew's readers to understand his use of family terminology, we should really look at Matthew 1:2, where we read: "Jacob generated Judah and his brothers." *But* who are his brothers? Reuben, Simeon, Levi, Issachar, and Zebulun, but he also has six brothers of a different mother. Together they constitute all his brothers and the twelve tribes of Israel. These two kinds of brethren constitute the two Biblical meanings of "brother" from the very onset of the New Testament. The first book of the New Testament or the first Gospel, in its first chapter, in its very first lines, sets the stage for the readers of Matthew (Mark, Luke, John, Acts, and Galatians) to understand exactly the range for a brother of Jesus. Matthew is setting the stage for us, throughout the New Testament, to see Jesus's brothers (and sisters/brethren) either as biological siblings in the fullest sense, or as brothers of a different mother. As we saw, intra-Biblical evidence makes it almost beyond doubt that Jesus's brethren are simply from another mother (unless they are more distant cousins as was just admitted above).

Also, Matthew occasionally concentrates in his list on a patrilineal figure like Jacob, but this leads him to exclude both of Jacob's wives when mentioning *him*. Why? Wives are mentioned to show a pattern of women who have a very

---

[43] Of course, there is yet another traditional reading where Joseph was married twice, but his first wife already had children and she died without consummation of their union; whereas Joseph died without consummation of his union with his second wife Mary. As obvious, this constitutes an even more complex and unlikely, if possible, read of the data.

limited number of children, whose names are all known in Matthew chapter 1. When the mothers are excluded, then and only then do we see the patrilineal line mentioning brothers and sisters. As Jacob had from his seed all of his own biological children, it is nonetheless true that these were from more than one wife. Matthew clearly wishes to ignore this fact. Instead, he emphasizes that *Joseph's* line had men who possessed more than one wife but whose children were brethren or brothers, even if they were of a different mother; like Judah and his full and half-brothers.[44] Matthew's list seems clearly to work like a decoder ring to understand what is happening in Matthew's (and even Mark's) Gospel: Joseph's blended family lives at the house of Nazareth, whereupon Joseph's death, his daughters of his first marriage (stereotypically) went wild and became notorious for their opposition to Jesus and they served to undercut Jesus's claim to prophethood in the eyes of the Nazarene community.

Matthew additionally related an historical pattern that was meant to contextualize Joseph's patrilineal record: Notice, Abraham had two wives, Sarah and Hagar.[45] The first wife Sarah was second to conceive the main child of blessing (Isaac). Jacob had two wives where Rachel was the second to bear a first-born only son, Joseph. Judah strangely begot his twins from a woman (Tamar) married to two husbands who were both dead. Then, we see in the cases of the females Tamar and Rehab that these ostensibly dishonorable prostitutes become heroines or

---

[44] This connection was first made by Eusebius, *Ecclesiastical History*, 84 (book 2, chapter 1).

[45] This notion is controversial. Paul (Galatians 4:24-24) does not endorse Hagar as a true wife but may imply it by admitting that her allegorized children are children of "a covenant" and "according to the flesh" which is used to describe Jesus's legitimate lineage in Romans 1:3. Rabbinic literature speaks ambiguously of her as "bound" to Abraham. However, Sumerian and cuneiform texts assure us that, at the time and locale of Abraham, a slave who bore the household father a male heir had the ability to become a legal wife by that very fact. This seems to be the custom here. Furthermore, this may be implied in Genesis 21:9-12, to the extent that Sarah fears that –although Isaac is conceived by a miracle– Ishmael has a right to the inheritance of Abraham. Only by driving away Ishmael and the mother does she eliminate the threat that Ishmael has rights in the household. This suggests that Hagar has the status of a wife *because* she produced male offspring for Abraham.

honorably established members of the Israelite community.[46] This clearly sets an ancestral example for Joseph to reflect and be cautious about assuming that his second wife, Mary, is unfaithful and dishonorable. Mary, the second wife to Joseph the widower, shortly after their engagement is thought by Joseph in his mental musings to be an adulteress. But he should know better: thinking about the lot of Tamar, Rahab, and Bathsheba; they are all celebrated women who contribute to the building up of Israel. So, before a scandal comes about, God intervenes and justifies Mary likewise before Joseph. Thus, all questions about the honor of Joseph and Mary strengthening Jesus's prophethood in Mark chapter 6 and Matthew chapter 13 become moot; so that Jesus refuses whether implicitly, or explicitly, to grant their inclusion into the list of non-honored and dishonorable persons cited by his enemies, as if these honorable persons could never per se impede the Nazareth community from accepting him.

Before exploring the household or patrilineal house of Joseph in Nazareth, it is worthwhile resolving and age-old problem continuously brought up by scholars, namely, "Why is Nazareth so important a part of Matthew's prophecy"? Generally speaking, there is anything from a scholarly denial that Matthew cites Scripture, to criticism of his citation, to confusion about Matthew 2:23: "And he went and lived in a town called Nazareth. So was fulfilled what was said through the prophets, that he would be called a Nazarene." Let us look at the real prophecies, which are twofold: by the Angel named Wonderful to Samson's mother and the Word of the Lord to Isaiah:

Genesis 16:11	LXX Genesis 16:11:
Behold you will have and conceive a son in your womb **and shall call his name** ISHMAEL, because the Lord was attentive to your lowliness-humility.	Ἰδοὺ σὺ ἐν γαστρὶ ἔχεις καὶ τέξῃ υἱὸν **καὶ καλέσεις τὸ ὄνομα αὐτοῦ ΙΣΜΑΗΛ** [whom God hears] ὅτι ἐπήκουσεν κύριος τῇ ταπεινώσει σου.
Judges 13:5, Judges 13:24:	Judges 13:5, Judges 13:24:
Behold you will have in your womb and conceive and he will take up a razor upon his head because THE	ἰδοὺ σὺ ἐν γαστρὶ ἕξεις καὶ τέξῃ υἱόν καὶ οὐκ ἀναβήσεται σίδηρος ἐπὶ τὴν κεφαλὴν αὐτοῦ ὅτι

---

[46] This pattern is less precisely noticed in Brown, *Mary in the New Testament*, 78.

CHILD/SON BELONGING TO GOD [Hebrew = *BÊN ELOHIM*: SON OF GOD] SHALL BE HALLOWED, as a Naz/rite from his womb, and he will begin **to save Israel** from the hands of foreigners […] and **she called his name** SAMSON [a deliverer of Israel].	ἩΓΙΑΣΜΕΝΟΝ ναζιραῖον ἔσται ΤΩΙ ΘΕΩΙ ΤΟ ΠΑΙΔΑΡΙΟΝ ἐκ τῆς γαστρός, καὶ αὐτὸς ἄρξεται **σώζειν τὸν Ισραηλ** ἐκ χειρὸς ἀλλοφύλων […] **καὶ ἐκάλεσεν τὸ ὄνομα αὐτοῦ** ΣΑΜΨΩΝ [a deliverer of Israel] […]
Isaiah 7:14	LXX Isaiah 7:14
Yahweh himself shall give a sign: Behold the virgin will receive and conceive in her womb a son, **and you shall call his name IMMANUEL**	δώσει κύριος αὐτὸς ὑμῖν σημεῖον· ἰδοὺ ἡ παρθένος ἐν γαστρὶ ἕξει καὶ τέξεται υἱόν, **καὶ καλέσεις τὸ ὄνομα αὐτοῦ EMMANOYHΛ·**
Matthew 1:21, 2:22:	Matthew 1:21-23 2:22:
And you shall call his name JESUS [he will save], for **he will save his people** from their sins. All this happened so that the saying should be fulfilled by the Lord saying that through the prophet: "Behold the virgin will have and conceive a son in her womb, and they will call his name IMMANUEL. […] and **she called his name JESUS** […] and he went to dwell in the city called Nazareth, with the result that what was spoken through the prophets be fulfilled, namely, "he shall be called a NazOrene "	**καὶ καλέσεις τὸ ὄνομα αὐτοῦ** ἸΗΣΟΥΝ (translated: he will save), αὐτὸς γὰρ **σώσει τὸν λαὸν αὐτοῦ** ἀπὸ τῶν ἁμαρτιῶν αὐτῶν. Τοῦτο δὲ ὅλον γέγονεν ἵνα πληρωθῇ τὸ ῥηθὲν ὑπὸ κυρίου διὰ τοῦ προφήτου λέγοντος, Ἰδοὺ ἡ παρθένος ἐν γαστρὶ ἕξει καὶ τέξεται υἱόν, **καὶ καλέσουσιν τὸ ὄνομα αὐτοῦ ἘMMANOYHΛ**, ὅ ἐστιν μεθερμηνευόμενον **Μεθ' ἡμῶν ὁ θεός.** [...]**καὶ ἐκάλεσεν τὸ ὄνομα αὐτοῦ** ἸΗΣΟΥΝ [...] καὶ ἐλθὼν κατῴκησεν εἰς πόλιν λεγομένην Ναζαρέτ, ὅπως πληρωθῇ τὸ ῥηθὲν διὰ τῶν προφητῶν ὅτι Ναζωραῖος κληθήσεται.
Luke 1:26, 31-32, 35:	Luke 1:26, 31-32, 35:

Gabriel [went ...] in the city called ^{Nazareth} to a virgin betrothed to a man; the virgin's name was Mary [...] Behold you will receive in your womb and conceive a son **and shall call his name JESUS**. This one shall be called great and A SON OF THE MOST HIGH [...] **he shall be called** HOLY.	Γαβριὴλ [...] εἰς πόλιν τῆς Γαλιλαίας ᾗ ὄνομα Ναζαρὲθ πρὸς παρθένον ἐμνηστευμένην ἀνδρὶ ᾧ ὄνομα τῆς παρθένου Μαριάμ. [...] ἰδοὺ συλλήμψῃ ἐν γαστρὶ καὶ τέξῃ υἱόν, **καὶ καλέσεις τὸ ὄνομα αὐτοῦ ΙΗΣΟΥΝ**. Οὗτος ἔσται μέγας καὶ ΥΙΟΣ ΥΨΙΣΤΟΥ ΚΛΗΘΗΣΕΤΑΙ [...] ΑΓΙΟΝ κληθήσεται

Wow! Samson, it is true, seems to be something like the warrior-child of Hagar, but this merely makes Samson the mediator between Abraham's seed and the New Testament. How can scholarly commentaries dismiss out of hand the typological reading of Judges 13:5 (typological means: Old Testament historical event acts as a model for an even more impressive or grace-filled New Testament event fulfilling something lacking in the old event for salvation)? It's very obvious, even if Biblical experts are entirely disinterested in Matthew's and Luke's shared conviction (quoting the annunciation to Samson's mother and Samson's conception) that the superhuman Samson and his conception form the model to understand typologically the child of promise who is coming to save the world!

Allegedly, the infancy narratives between Matthew and Luke are said to be entirely different, even contradictory by naysayers. This is simply not so. Each author is clearly developing either the Joseph-side or the Mary-side of the same prophecies and same story as a fulfillment of a type: the "New Samson" (compare Judges chapter 13). The fact is that in all the Gospels, save Mark, the only common adjective by which Gospel writers in Antiquity universally heard Greek speakers identify a person from Nazareth was by the adjective: "**NazOrene**." Would that Matthew have had sources or knowledge for the alternative term: **NazArene** (*Nazarênos*) known peculiarly to Mark, since Mark's wordplay on Judges' is more obvious: **NazIrene/NazIrite** (*Naziraios*). Outside of Galilean dialect, or Hebrew, or an Aramaic pun, Mark's Greek term would have gotten the reader very close to the original wordplay, obviously enjoyed by hearers of the joke-by-prophecy, known to the compiler of the prophetic material used by the (synoptic) Gospel writers. What we can conclude now straightforwardly is that there is a prophecy in both Matthew and Luke, namely, the Angel who counseled (Angel of Great

Council; LXX Isaiah 9:6) Manoah and Samson's mom is Yahweh himself and he is discovered to have the name "Wonderful," (MT Judges 13:18), just like Jesus in his mother's womb is referred to likewise as an Angel of Lord or "Wonderful" (MT Genesis 18:14; Isaiah 9:5-6) in Luke 1:37, citing LXX Genesis 18:14.

1.4 The Brothers and Sisters of Jesus in Matthew Chapter 13

We have seen Mark's skillful organization of material in order to talk about Mary's role in his Gospel. Some of the same material was available to Matthew. For his part, Matthew decides to tell the story differently. He wants to use a back and forth motion: **Jesus goes out**, **Jesus goes in**, then **Jesus goes out and in**, arriving, thereafter, at his familiar *fatherland/homeland* in Matthew chapter 13:

[A₁] On the same day Jesus **went out** of [α] the house and sat by the sea. ² And great multitudes were gathered together to him, so that he got into a boat and sat; and the whole multitude stood on the shore.

   [B₁] Jesus preaches [α] publicly a parable

[A₂] ³⁶ Then Jesus sent the multitude away and **went into** [β] the house. And his disciples came to him, saying, "Explain to us the parable of the tares of the field."

   [B₂] Jesus teaches [β] privately a parable

   [Conclusion:] ⁵¹ Jesus said to them, "Have you understood all these things?" They said to Him, "Yes, Lord." ⁵² Then He said to them, "Therefore every scribe instructed concerning the kingdom of heaven is like a [β] pater_familias_/Lord-of-the-manor (*oikodespôtês*) who brings out of his treasure things new and old." [Joseph = honorable]

[A.₃] ⁵³ Now it came to pass, when Jesus had finished these parables, that **He departed** from there. ⁵⁴ When **He had come**

   [B₃] *to His own country*, [α] He taught them in their SYNAGOGUE, so that they were astonished and said, "Where did this man get

51

this ₍wisdom₎ and THESE MIGHTY WORKS? ⁵⁵ Is this not the carpenter's [Joseph's] son? Is not his mother called Mary? And his brothers James, Joses, Simon, and Judas? ⁵⁶ And his sisters, are they not all [β] with us? Where then did this man get all these things?" ⁵⁷ So they were offended at him. But Jesus said to them,

[B₄] "A prophet is not without honor except *in his own country* and [β] in his own house." ⁵⁸ Now, he did not do MANY MIGHTY WORKS there because of their ₍unbelief₎.

[A₁] **Jesus went** out of a house into public and things went well! We are starting to see in Mark and now Matthew that when Jesus *goes privately into* a house [A₂ B₄] things can get messy. Normally, people in Jesus' house are problematic. Notice here, however, that his disciples "follow" him into the house. Therefore, their belief, though with some initial problems, will vindicate them since they did *follow him* into the house. They ultimately get over the bad fortune of family in his *private house* so that, conversely, his disciples listen and then do God's will. They are a little dense, but they ultimately are good guys after Jesus sees them open to instruction. If α represents "going out into public" and β "in his own house," then notice the transition from [B₂], where Jesus sees that disciples get the correct way of thinking of the kingdom of God. It is at that moment that an oblique reference is made by Jesus to his own household where somebody had once gotten a treasure for embracing the kingdom.

A puzzle (if not alleged contradiction) repeated by the scholar Rev. Dr. Brown is solved by paying attention to this:[47] Scholars, discussing the infancy narrative in Matthew chapters 1-2, find it problematic that Joseph seems to have "a house" in Bethlehem (Matthew 2:10; "magi going into [Joseph's] house (*eis tên oikian*)"). After all, Joseph's real house in Mark and Luke should be uniquely in Nazareth. Why say that Joseph has "a house" in Bethlehem? Well, we have an obvious literary answer. This "house" is where something new was brought out of an old-Davidic house; the old-new house of Joseph. It is really easy to follow: Joseph took Jesus to "the house of David" Joseph's own household in Bethlehem.[48]

---

[47] Brown, *Mary in the New Testament*, 14.

[48] It is furthermore somewhat astonishing that scholars do not see that this solution is also presented in Luke 2:5: "And Joseph went up from the city of Nazareth in Galilee

52

There, Joseph saw magi presenting treasure to Jesus, worshipping him as the new king of Israel. By Joseph obediently going to his old house to listen to the prophecy of an angel, he occasioned the presentation of treasure in his ancestral house of Bethlehem to the new king, the New David of Israel! There is no contradiction or mistake here, but an obvious play on the fact that Joseph of the ancient house of David (Matthew 1:20: "[Angel announces:] o Joseph, son of David") temporarily returns home to Bethlehem (= Hebrew *Beth* = house), dwelling in his patrilineal "house," out of which old house comes something newly revealed at the moment of receiving gold, frankincense and myrrh! However, Joseph's other house at Nazareth is seemingly full of Joseph's naughty extended family. Though once head of the household (paterfamilias) at Nazareth, Joseph had long before his death embraced the kingdom of God by obeying his dream at the opening of Matthew's Gospel at the house of David his father!

What is interesting here is that Matthew transitions Jesus out of another country to his own fatherland by a saying of Jesus that: "An Old Testament scholar" teaching about "the kingdom of God" is like the father of the household, who brings from his "treasure" what are new and what are old. "Treasure" is a big deal with Matthew (2:11; 6:19-21; 12:35; 13:44; 13:52; 19:21). But the only father of a house who is associated with treasure in Matthew is Joseph (Matthew 2:11)! The magi go into the dwelling or extended family household (*eis tên oikian*) of Joseph (son of David), take out gold, incense, and myrrh. In fact, Matthew 2:23 ends with speaking about Joseph (and Mary's) settling in Nazareth, which brings us full circle in Matthew 13:57, where Jesus finds himself again in his fatherland and house of Joseph. However, unlike Mark 6:1-6, Joseph is explicitly referred to in Matthew 13:55. What can be the possible meaning? If Mark 6:3 only mentions Mary (omitting Joseph the carpenter), which underlines the fact that Joseph is not around and Mary is a widow, then what does it mean that Joseph is obliquely named here in Matthew 13:54 as a carpenter? First, scholars know that the enemies of Jesus underline that he is a manual laborer to scorn him.[49] Secondly, they believe Joseph to be his biological father. Why doesn't Matthew correct the dishonor toward Joseph or to Mary or to Jesus's brothers but only refers dishonor to "his own house" or extended family of females? In answer, Matthew has already exonerated Joseph and Mary! Matthew chapters 1-2, or the virgin birth, means that

---

into Judah, to a city of David that is called Bethlehem, for because of the fact that he [Joseph] was from the house (*oikou*) and patrilineal descent (*patrias*) of David."

[49] Brown, *Mary in the New Testament*, 61.

Jesus's enemies are nothing to worry about. First, Joseph can be named as "son of Joseph" since Matthew (unlike Mark) has prepared us to understand that the list by Jesus's enemies does not accurately describe Jesus's paternity. There can be no confusion in Matthew. If Mark had done so, he would need to explain how Jesus does not have Joseph as a biological father (under the assumption that Mark knows the virgin-birth prophecy material to which Matthew and Luke have access). Mark has other worries in his Gospel, since any inclusion of Joseph's name (absent in Mark) demands an explanation. Since Jesus never directly responded to the accusations against Joseph in the source-material quoted by Mark and Matthew, Mark used one strategy: omit Joseph altogether from the list. Matthew used another strategy: talk about Joseph cooperating with the virgin birth at the beginning of the Gospel. For Mark, Matthew's solution brings about too much concentration on the biological (versus new kingdom of God) family of Jesus, a real political problem in the early church. The solution for Mark is simply to remove the name of Joseph altogether, or any reference to him as "the carpenter," while Matthew's solution is to prime the reader in his infancy narrative to know the accusation against Joseph is false in virtue of Joseph's honorable role in the virgin birth at the beginning of his Gospel!

Finally, note that Jesus's enemies in Matthew 13:55 follow up their mention of Joseph or the carpenter by calling Jesus strangely, the son of Mary! Should not Jesus's identity by now be obvious, as son of the town carpenter? Well, obvious it would be…unless Joseph had more than one wife! Listing both parents in succession makes no sense in a Jewish context! The most obvious way to read *Mark* is that Mary there is a widow. However, the most obvious way to read *Matthew* is to clarify from which of two wives of Joseph Jesus comes, *either* from his first, *or* from his second wife. While polygamy would be thinkable, the first-century evidence for polygamy in Romanized Palestine militates against it being probable. We are likely dealing with Joseph the widower, just as the first-century document the *Protevangelium* attests: "I already have sons (*hious*) and I am an old man."[50] The brothers and sisters are of another mother but of the same putative father of a patrilineal house; namely, of Joseph of Nazareth, the carpenter. Nonetheless, even though less likely in the context of Matthew, a rather incredulous explanation might be that Mary is the living mother of Jesus, while Joseph is the deceased father. Perhaps, if Joseph had died many years ago, his name would no longer even be remembered by villagers. But this sounds

---

[50] *Protoevangelium*, 48-49.

farfetched. Of course, this reading would favor the late-Latin tradition that Joseph was an unmarried man prior to wedding Mary. "Son of Joseph" or "Son of the carpenter" should easily identify Jesus, a famous miracle worker, in his small town where everybody knew everybody. This makes Matthew's seemingly unnecessary phrase: "son of Mary," unlike the rest of the Old and New Testament. It should be enough that the man of the house who has but one wife is sufficient to name as the parent in order to identify Jesus. Instead, Jesus's mother additionally must be named lest we make a mistake … What mistake? … The mistake –in all probability– of thinking Jesus is son of Joseph's first wife.

Matthew, then, confirms for us Mark's doctrine that this is the carpenter's <u>house</u>, where the sisters of Jesus live. These female relatives of Jesus belong to the patrilineal or extended family of Jesus under the protection of Joseph, or the carpenter with whom the house in <u>Nazareth</u> is identified. What is also awesome is that Matthew preserves an extra hint that he is aware of LXX Numbers 1:1-3, showing that both Mark and Matthew (not to mention Luke) are familiar with the Greek version of Numbers and its description of how to talk about Jewish families. Matthew playfully remarks that Jesus went to his homeland, but immediately entered "THE SYNAGOGUE." LXX Numbers 1:1-3 speaks of all Israel being a great ASSEMBLY or CONGREGATION or SYNAGOGUE. Secondly, we see the familiar distinctions: broadest: fatherland, less broad: kinsmen (of a different mother), broad: patrilineal extended family members, and least broad: (male) child Jesus of (Joseph-the-head and) Mary. The sources for Mark and Matthew on family divisions are clearly the same. If, however, we were left *only* with Matthew, and did not have Jesus's definitive proof that his brothers and sisters can be grouped together as relatives (*syngeneis*), or children of another mother by Jesus's own words in Mark, it is possible that a slightly greater amount of ambiguity in the passage above would remain; though LXX Numbers 1:1-2 seems to remove most doubt in this regard. Fortunately, too, Matthew actually clarifies an ambiguity that we saw in Mark 6:3. Remember, the list by Jesus's enemies included Jesus's relatives from another mother, who were not the same as his sisters causing trouble <u>in Nazareth</u> for him. I suggested that other references to Jesus's family following him around in Mark mean that Jesus only agreed that James, Joses, Judas, and Simon were not *honorific* or famous enough to make Jesus's family notable, *insofar as* they were nothing special as regards their status among contemporary Jews. They were not, however, Jesus's enemies, for how would he have made them an example of the classes of family who "do God's will" in Mark 3:32? Matthew 13:57 seems to confirm this, for just as Mary is omitted from those who bring dishonor to Jesus by Jesus's own list in Mark 6:4, so Matthew omits Jesus's relatives from Jesus's own listing of dishonorable persons and more strenuously links unbelief exclusively to the extended family in Jesus's local household.[51] As if the foregoing is not enough information, we should like to close our discussion by a quick reference to Matthew 10:34-36. This only serves to further solidify the arguments from Mark and Matthew until present. What we learn in Matthew chapter 10 is that Jesus himself refers to the technical family divisions (like Numbers) when speaking about intra-familial strife. To do so, Jesus quotes LXX Micah 7:6: "For son (*huion*) dishonors father, daughter rises against her mother, daughter-in-law (*nymphên*) against her mother-in-law; a man's enemies are the men of his own household." Notice that Jesus wishes to identify first-century households of non-believing Jews with familial structures known in the Bible. We notice that the mother of the bride or mother-in-law are part of the same household (*oikos*). Consequently, we find some pertinent information in Jesus speaking in Matthew 10:35-36: "For I have come to 'set a man (*anthrôpon*) against his father, a daughter against her mother, and a daughter-in-law (*nymphên*) against her mother-in-law'; and 'a man's enemies will be those of his own household (*oikiakoi*).'" Again, not only should we account half-sisters in Jesus's household, but perhaps Mary's mother-in-law or Joseph's mom as one of those who were resistant to the message of Jesus at his home. Notice that, if this is plausible, Mary is identified as opposed by her mother-in-law. The mother of Joseph would then have dissensions with her granddaughters (likely from Joseph's first marriage). But notice that Jesus is not shown to quote Micah perfectly: Instead of Jesus claiming (by implication) that he and Joseph (son and father per Micah) are in opposition, Jesus more generically refers to "a man being" set against his father. This could be taken as Jesus distancing himself from physical ancestry directly from Joseph's natural seed (because of the virgin birth). However, this would mean that Matthew forgot that Joseph supported Jesus in Matthew chapter 1-2, or that he did a poor job editing his source materials. More likely to me, it seems that Jesus' is referring to any male head (*kephalê*) who in general lives in the household and who is at odds with the paterfamilias. Jesus contrasting his language to the citation from Micah who he is referring to a biological son. This would argue that

---

[51] See *Protoevangelium*, 9.9-10, where Joseph objects to marrying Mary. This is significant because this refusal to enter into a second marriage forebodes a punishment that he will now have a divided family. The commentator possibly alludes to the disruptive sisters of Jesus in Joseph's household as a temporal punishment by God for Joseph's hesitating to marry Mary after he was chosen by lot.

Jesus's support in his house are from Joseph and Mary who were often fighting with Joseph's mom, Joseph's girls (likely daughters from his first marriage), and that the dishonorable girls (gone wild) after Joseph's death not only disagree with Jesus and Mary, but with their grandmother whom they annoy as well. What is the motive? In all of this we see that the females other than Mary in Joseph's household are apparently prone to resist the Gospel and cause dissension even to the shedding of blood if possible.

Concluding remarks:

In every way, Matthew complements Mark, and to a very limited extent, Matthew even supplements our information on Joseph's and Jesus's family, if only we read the Scriptures paying close attention to its technical vocabulary, wordplays, and authors' reliance on previous Scripture. Matthew uses his own storytelling genius to speak on the very same issue as the presumably older account of Mark. However, both seem to have a very primitive set of sources that suggest much of what they are concerned with deals with a Judaism before the destruction of the Temple, though we can admit that Jewish theology and interpretation of history needed time even after the destruction of Jerusalem to adjust to its new reality. That said, we also see Matthew making in general only a sort of barebones mention of Mary's role among her family members. We can only glean that, in harmony with Mark, Mary needs to be exempted from the list of dishonorable persons in Jesus's family who bring him no honor in his homeland. However, Matthew earlier provided obvious reasons why his interpretation is such: Matthew chapters 1-2 clearly intend to set the stage for Matthew in a way that Mark did not feel inspired to do. Matthew wanted to start including Mary's younger life, especially her virgin birth and her honorable maidenhood, as an introduction to other materials commonly known between Mark and Matthew that mention her in difficult family situations. At this point, what becomes obvious is the fact that Mary and Joseph bring no dishonor on Jesus in Matthew 13:55; for that reason Jesus does not include oblique or explicit references to them when speaking about the family members who do dishonor him. We also saw that this reading is not only secure because of Mark and Matthew's application of the family structure of LXX Numbers 1:1-3 to Jesus's family tree, but Joseph and Mary are portrayed as persons giving Jesus extrinsic honor by their faith and manner of life in chapters 1-2 of Matthew. The net result is that Matthew is ambivalent about the nature of dishonor that is imputed to Jesus due to his relatives from another mother. This in no way necessitates that Matthew agrees that Jesus's brothers/cousins (*adelphoi/syngeneis*) are dishonorable and, like Mark, he can imply that they are persons of little importance or of little gravity for their testimony among those living in Jesus's obscure and backwater town. Mark, on the other hand, reproduces a fuller amount of material regarding Jesus's description of his kinsmen, who followed him around; these might not be honorific at Nazareth, but they were worthy nonetheless to be called *Jesus's brothers and mothers* (Mark 3:32); unlike Jesus's stay-at-home female extended family at Nazareth. In the end, Matthew 13:53-58 is all about Jesus's dramatic return home after divine, if secret, honors have already been bestowed on his mother and (deceased) carpenter-father from about thirty years prior to his arrival at Nazareth.

Chapter Two:

Mary in the Gospel of Luke

2.1 Blessed Hearing of the Word of God and Believing in Luke Chapters 1:1-3

After completing our enjoyable tour through the older Gospels of Matthew and Mark, a classic place to begin puzzling about Mary in Luke lies in the seemingly disparaging and classically contested passages of this heavily *Marian* Gospel: "As Jesus was saying these things, a woman in the crowd called out, '**Blessed** (*makaria*) is the mother who gave you birth and nursed you.' He replied, '**Blessed** (*makarioi*) rather are those *who hear* **the word** (*ton logon*) of God and keep it'" (Luke 11:27-28). For many English speakers, these verses appear at first glance to slight Mary and lead to the understandable question why a Bible-based Christian would give Mary honor without reserve. Despite Luke's praises of Mary elsewhere, Jesus initially appears to want distance himself from Mary's maternity, or does he?

As usual, our lack of understanding the Bible's framework or context (that is, first-century Greek Christianity) prevents us from easily making sense of this passage, especially in English translation. Greek-speaking Christian compilers of the Bible into "lectionaries" or Sunday-service books organized Scripture selections that started to become pretty fixed by around 600 AD, even if the oldest feasts had fixed readings well before in the fourth centuries from what we can tell from people like John Chrysostom and his homilies. The lectionaries or biblical readings for church services were used for shouting and singing aloud at services the Scriptures. Occasionally, the compiler throws us for a loop by his selections: The lectionary compiler doesn't always give us a continuous chapter and verse reading day-by-day. In this vein, the way that a compiler of service-book readings combines different passages into a composite Gospel is sometimes a hint at an interpretation that the compiler values, where one selection or pericope is complementary or supplementary to another. The Greek-speaking compiler of the Byzantine lectionary for the feast of the entrance of the child Mary into the Temple (November 21) found a key to discovering who these unnamed people are "who hear the word of God and keep it." Before we touch on the Gospel reading for the ancient feast of the "Entrance of the Theotokos" or "Presentation of Mary in the Temple," we should turn to Luke who tells us at the beginning of his Gospel (Luke 1:1-3):

> Many have undertaken to draw up an account of the things […] as they were handed down to us by those who from the first were eyewitnesses and servants of **the word** (*tou logou*) […] I myself have carefully investigated everything from the beginning, I too decided to write an orderly account […] so that you may know the security of **the words** (*logôn*) regarding which you were catechized.

In the first century AD, Luke wants us to infer that Mary is the witness interviewed for details about her pregnancy, birth, and some facts about Jesus's infancy. We also notice that Christians are supposed to be "servants of **the word**" as people "catechized in **the word**." Obviously, Mary alone would have been present for the first event of the Annunciation, while the latter two events were unlikely to have been related to Luke by the presumably much older Joseph, demonstrably dead by the time of Jesus's crucifixion, as per our discussions in Mark and Matthew. This already portends a "Marian" angle to Luke's storytelling of the Gospel. Now that the Jews have been defeated, killed, and their survivors captured and exiled in Jerusalem, the family monopoly on the church in Jerusalem was apparently broken, as Hegessipus mentioned to us in his second-century history of the Christian church. So, Mary in Luke's post-destruction Gospel lives in a church where the apostles had finally wrested control of Palestinian Christianity from Jesus's relatives who were constantly a source of tension, not only for Jesus, but for the rest of the church, as all four Gospels mention. They were enshrined in church history (and this squares with the Evangelists designating them to be troublemakers) as people trying to capitalize on their genetic bloodline as their claim to church leadership, instead of the charisms of the spirit and the apostolic succession, whereby Jesus often chose persons not related to him by blood to represent him to his community after his ascension. Of course, only a minority of these leaders were his blood relations. So, Luke's story is a new interpretation of the same scene that was already studied in Mark (3:31–34) in chapter 1.

Mark was already very close to Luke's point that to be blessed is not principally or morally a matter of biological conceiving or physical lactating but of responding to a call or to knowledge of what God wants someone to do. Still,

Jesus leaves us with the potential impression that he's not excited to see a crowd of people identified first with his mom, then with his relatives. In fact, the latest Gospel is closest to the time when Church historians tell us that Jesus's blood relatives were trying to thwart the church in virtue of their DNA. We read (John 7:5): "For even his own brothers did not believe in him." Gospel writers from Mark to John sometimes emphasize the dishonorable moments (even if they don't totally ignore honorable cousins and familiars of Jesus) with respect to his biological family. As Eusebius reminds us around AD 300 (citing historians who lived earlier), there was constant tension whereby the relatives of Jesus tried to ride on his coattails in from around AD 30 onward, or they raised their own family always to seek positions of honor, causing trouble for the apostles and the Evangelists who wanted to convey that leaders of the Church were frequently not blood relations of Jesus.[52] *Now that we have the first century mindset,* we can understand the tension prior to the first destruction of Jerusalem in AD 70, whose remnants even affected the church until the second destruction of the Jewish nation at the Simon Bar Kochba rebellion (AD 132-136). Only after this time do preoccupations about Jesus's blood relatives trying to cash in on Jesus's stardom come to a tragic end by death, enslavement, or exile from the Jerusalem Church by pagan Roman violence.

2.2 Mary Hears the Word of God and Keeps It in Luke 1:29-45

One of Luke's prophecy fulfillments is to show the relation between the antetypes or imperfect historical anticipations of Jesus and Mary; namely, Abraham and Sarah and how their New Testament realities fulfill perfectly prophecy of Abraham having a child who, besides Isaac, shall be called "(too) Wonderful" (Genesis 18:14), clearly a hint at something greater than the miracle-child born to Sarah. Abraham is the first figure to undergo the "annunciation-pattern" in the ancient history of salvation as a preparation for the real thing in the Roman empire under Augustus Caesar. Abraham's and Sarah's "lesser" annunciation in Genesis chapter 18 is pretty straightforward: (1.) Abraham is at his tent, (2.) He looks up, (3.) He sees a vision of three men who are one God by name, (4.) He falls down and he washes their feet and afterwards provides them with a

---

[52] Eusebius, *Ecclesiastical History*, 59-65 (book I, chapter 7).

meal under the shadow of the oak of Mamre, (5.) Although Abraham is announced to have a child of promise, whom he understands to begin with Isaac, the prophecy widens to include numberless generations unto the future and cryptic mention by one of the three angels that there is something "(too) Wonderful" in comparison to Sarah's annunciation and miraculous pregnancy. Sarah gets the chance to respond appropriately to her announcement or annunciation at a tent, by the angels, about a child of promise. But she is rebuked for being in some way less than credulous about having sexual activity to bear a child. As such, we get the impression that the annunciation didn't go as well as it could have, and that Sarah missed out on an opportunity for perfect faith like Abraham.

In Luke chapter 1, we see that Zachariah, similar to Sarah undergoes an annunciation by a (created) angel and instead of immediately answering with faith, he answers with something less than trust, full-fledged doubt. His rebuke leads the angel to mute his ability to speak from his announcement or annunciation until the naming of the precursor prophet John who shall announce the child named "(too) Wonderful." The all-important point here is finally manifest, the angel accused him, not unlike Sarah (Luke 1:20): "You did not believe in my **word(s)** (*ouk episteusas tois logois mou*)." The first person to whom the word or words of the Lord in Luke's Gospel came and were heard is by someone who does *not* keep them!

Luke expects us, when getting to the Gospel (11:28), already to apply the answer key for the question: "Who are the ones who hear the word and keep it?" After all, the reader wants to be blessed like them! Well, we must read on to find out even more: Next, we turn to Mary. The angel tells her (using the Septuagint reading of Genesis 18:14), that a child called "Wonderful" will be born with the name of Jesus and that she is to be the mother by a miraculous Sarah-like conception but of an even more impossible manner; the manner predicted in Judges chapter 13 and Isaiah 7:14; namely of both a Nazarite and of a virgin (from her youth with a perpetual Nazarite vow common to the New Testament period); she will bear the one called "Wonderful." Like Abraham, a shadow —or rather overshadowing— will mark the place where Mary meets the Trinity of persons, but this overshadowing is predicted to happen by Gabriel *inside* Mary's womb, unlike Sarah whose distant view of overshadowing was *outside*. What is the response of Mary? It is a puzzled but faithful "yes," which is found pleasing to God. The key is as follows (Luke 1:29): "[Having heard,][53] she was disturbed by **the word** and **reasoned** about what kind of greeting [from Gabriel] this could be (*hê de epi tôi logôi dietarachthê kai dielog*izeto potapos eiê o asposmos outos*)." She heard the **word** of the Lord and kept it! As such, she was inspired to sing her own praises, prophetically honored by Elizabeth in the presence of the embryonic Christ, and finally at Jesus's birth. She then gave her breasts for him to suck by the baby Jesus, which leads to this phrase of our Gospeler Luke: "Mary guarded all these reports (namely what the angels **spoke/worded** (*legontôn*) [*angelôn*]), "storing them up in her heart" (Luke 2:19, 51).[54] When the prophetess Elizabeth recounts by the Holy Spirit what happened at the Annunciation, Elizabeth utters: "**Blessed** is she who believed (*makaria hê pisteusasa*)" (Luke 1:45). Mary reechoes her prophetic cousin by her own song of praise: "For behold, from now on, all generations **shall call** me **blessed** (*makarioūsin*)" (Luke 1:48).

---

[53] See Robert Weber, Roger Gryson (eds.), *Biblia sacra iuxta vulgatam versionem* (Stuttgart: Deutsche Bibelgesellschaft, 2007), 1606. This is a variant attested in the Latin Vulgate of Jerome: "*cum audisset.*" It does not merit mention in the Nestle-Aland critical edition in Greek and is assuredly inauthentic in Jerome's original edition. I add it because it is a fascinating interpolation, where an Latin ancient copyist saw Mary to be the one who "first heard" and then "she believed." It is worthwhile underlining that this variant is also alluded to in Greek by the *Protevangelium*, 11.6: "But when *she heard* (*akousasa*), Mary was doubtful and said, 'If I actually conceive by the Lord the living God, will I also give birth the way women usually do?'"

[54] This insight is explicitly in Augustine of Hippo, *Of Holy Virginity*, in *St. Augustin: On the Holy Trinity, Doctrinal Treatises, Moral Treatises*, ed. P. Schaff, trans. C. L. Cornish (Buffalo, NY: Christian Literature Company 1887), 3:418:

Mary is more blessed in receiving the faith of Christ (Luke 1:46), than in conceiving the flesh of Christ (Luke 1:35). For to a certain one who said, "Blessed is the womb, which bare Thee" (Luke 11:27) He Himself made answer, "Yea, rather, blessed are they who hear the Word of God, and keep it" (Luke 11:28). Lastly, to His brethren, that is, His kindred after the flesh, who believed not in Him (John 7:5), what profit was there in that being of kin? Thus also her nearness as a Mother would have been of no profit to Mary, had she not borne Christ in her heart (Luke 2:19) after a more blessed manner than in her flesh.

The obvious conclusion that Jesus in Luke wants us to draw is that, "rather" (*menounge*)[55] than being blessed for a series of biological praises, Mary should, "yes, even more so" (*menoun*) be declared blessed as the first who heard the word and who then believed unlike Sarah and Zachariah. It was Mary's antecedent righteousness (unlike Abraham), being "full of grace" even before seeing an angel of the Lord, that ensured that she would make the best of all possible responses: "Hearing the word of God and keeping it." How did she become blessed? She became the mother of Jesus, the mother of the Savior, the mother of the messiah, God-man, Jesus Christ! If we take Luke to be expanding our information about Mark's Gospel (adding on some more recorded conversations), then we are even led to believe that anybody who hears Jesus and responds to the will of God will be honored in the same manner as Mary; namely, they will have a share in the graces she experienced as one full of grace.[56] We tend to identify this with justification or being in a state of righteousness, justice, and friendship with God. These conclusions merely fall in line with a similarly close patristic reading of the vocabulary and evidence by the polyglot scholar the Venerable Bede:

> But the woman pronounces blessed not only her who was thought worthy to give birth from her body to the **Word** of God, but those also who have desired by *the hearing* of faith spiritually to conceive the same **Word**, and by diligence in good works, either in their own or the hearts of their neighbors, to bring it forth and

---

[55] See Maurice Robinson and William Pierpont (eds.), *The New Testament in the Original Greek: Byzantine Text-Form 2018* (Nürnberg GE: VTR Publications, 2018), 179, where the Byzantine churches preserve this alternative reading: "*menounge*."

[56] John Chrysostom, who was not overly ready to exaggerate Mary's holiness, gives this interpretation, as can be found in Thomas Aquinas's, *Catena Aurea: Commentary on the Four Gospels*, Collected out of the Works of the Fathers: St. Luke, ed. J. H. Newman (Oxford: John Henry Parker, 1843), 3:409:

> In this answer He sought not to disown His mother, but to shew that His birth would have profited her nothing, had she not been really fruitful in works and faith. But if it profited Mary nothing that Christ derived His birth from her, without the inward virtue of her heart, much less will it avail us to have a virtuous father, brother, or son, while we ourselves are strangers to virtue. (*Homily 44: on Matthew*)

nourish it; for it follows, But he said, Yea rather, **blessed** are they that *hear* **the word** of God, and keep it.[57]

But she was the mother of God, and therefore indeed **blessed**, in that she was made the temporal minister of the Word becoming incarnate; yet therefore much more blessed that she remained the eternal keeper of the same ever to be beloved **Word**. But this expression startles the wise men of the Jews, who sought not *to hear* and keep the word of God, but to deny and blaspheme it.[58]

2.3 A Second Person to Hear the Word of God and Keep It in Luke 10:38-42

At this point, have we not proved out point beyond doubt? Isn't it more than obvious that Luke's Jesus was actually complimenting Mary by means of wordplays on "the word" and "keeping it"? Yet, we have one more point to make: The Byzantine or Eastern Roman empire used Greek in its church services and the Eastern Orthodox and Eastern Catholic churches of the Greek world still use the very same lectionary texts that started to get solidified around AD 600. But the Annunciation feast had likely been around since AD 448 in Constantinople (instituted perhaps by Archbishop Flavian) and was officially made a national and Church holiday on 25 March 560 by Emperor Justinian I. Because other Marian feasts (the more ancient ones) already read from large portions of Luke 1-2, the compiler of the edition of the lectionary that first included the feast of Mary's Presentation in the Temple or Entrance (around AD 700) at the capital of the Eastern Roman or Byzantine Church (Constantinople) likely wanted a fresh Gospel selection just for the Entry of the child Mary into the Temple. Hence, by making the same attentive reading of Luke's Gospel, notice what the compiler of

---

[57] See Aquinas, *Catena Aurea*, 3:408–409.

[58] See Aquinas, *Catena Aurea*, 3:409.

the service book does for the Mary-Gospel on November 21ˢᵗ; it's quite strange! The compiler gave selections weirdly as follows: Luke 10:38-42:

> As Jesus and his disciples were on their way, he came to a village where a woman named Martha opened her home to him. She had a sister called Mary, who sat at the Lord's feet and *heard* his **word** (*êkouen **ton logon***). But Martha was distracted by all the preparations that had to be made. She came to him and asked, "Lord, don't you care that my sister has left me to do the work by myself? Tell her to help me!" "Martha, Martha," the Lord answered, "you are worried and upset about many things, but few things are needed—or indeed only one. Mary has chosen what is better, and it will not be taken away from her."

Now the compiler jumps forward in the Evangeliary or lectionary-Gospel book to Luke 11:27-28:

> As Jesus was saying these things, a woman in the crowd called out, "Blessed is the mother who gave you birth and nursed you." He replied, "Yes, but even more:[59] Blessed are those *who hear* **the word** (*hoi akouontes **ton logon***) of God and keep it."[60]

Ah! We have now come full circle; the other major person named in honor of Mary (viz., Mary of Magdala) also heard the word of God and kept it undistracted! Like Mark's Gospel, she uses her "will" or "chooses" to be listening to Jesus's word. If all the good Mary-Gospel passages were already taken by the lectionary, could not this Medieval-Mary festival best choose this passage to fill out Luke's Marian Gospel exhortation by reading about Mary II or Mary of Magdala –imitating Mary I or Mary, mother of the God-man Jesus? However, a last puzzle remains: Luke is a bit of an "Atticizer" or a bit of a Greek grammarian. This means that we might expect a really clever Luke to be speaking about the two believing women earlier

---

[59] See Brown, *Mary in the New Testament*, 171. Brown notes that "rather" is typically used when there something corrective but this preferred translation would be valid, *if only it were clear that Jesus affirms or makes a positive statement*. In light of the evidence, we can safely conclude that Jesus simply made a modification of what the anonymous woman said previously by him so that she was *not incorrect*.

[60] If Luke wanted to speak about the *earlier women alone*, he would have wrote: "***makariai … hai akousasai*** (**blessed** are the ladies *who heard* […])."

in his Gospel by writing: "**Blessed** (*makariai*) are the lady-*hearers* (*hai akousai*) of the word of God who obey it." But this isn't Jesus's point here, is it? His point is that Mary, mother of Jesus, is the first of many disciples (e.g., Mary II) and that everybody (including men) at today's meeting with Jesus has the vocation to be a mini-Mary and receive her blessing of justification (oh, and Luke also gets his chance to get in an extra jab against those pesky DNA-fortune hunters still trying to run the church of Christ based upon their ancestry.com profile)![61]

Luke opens his entire Gospel hoping that any reader will key in on "**the word**" and "**the words**" to which a Christian is called to be the servant. Immediately following, Mary's dignity and vocation are unsurprisingly at the center of Luke's *Marian* Gospel, as the first servant of **the word** who holds at her Annunciation **the word** in her heart and chose the word in an act of will: "Let it be done to me." Elizabeth, under the influence of the Holy Spirit, prophetically recounts that this moment resulted in: "**Blessed** is she who believed (*makaria hê piseusasa*)" (Luke 1:45). Mary's merit was not in physical conception, *rather* (*menoun*) **blessed** is she who heard the word and believed! Mary proves to be the very key to understanding Luke's wordplays, then Mary II's vocation to the word repeats by wordplay a similar situation (though Mary II is *not* explicitly "**blessed**" like Mary), and finally we are even extended a participation in the Christian vocation to be mini-Marys in Christ by responding by our will in our knowledge of **the word** of God by faith or believing. The only people Luke wants to exclude from Jesus's happy place are his bossy relatives who try to capitalize over and against the apostles in virtue of the bitcoin known as their bloodline, as if church leadership

---

[61] The application of this verse to all men and women is an insight noticed as early as Ephrem the Syrian, *Commentary on Tatian's Diatesseron* (Downers Grove, IL: InterVarsity Press, 2005), 3:195:

"Blessed is the womb that bore you." He took blessedness from the one who bore him and gave it to those who were worshiping him. It was with Mary for a certain time, but it would be with those who worshiped him for eternity. "Blessed are those who hear the word of God and keep it."

were a birthright to tyrannize the early Church without either the charisms of the Spirit, or the personal election by Jesus, to lead his church.[62]

2.4 Annunciations: From *Protoevangelium* (Genesis 3:15) to Mary in Luke 1:37

The most ancient prophecy of a woman with a son who will bring peace to the enmity or war between humans and Satan by victory of the accuser or tempter of mankind is called the *Protoevangelium* or Pre-Gospel of the Book of Genesis. We know the story that when Eve sins, she and her accuser, the serpent, are formally declared enemies. However, both the Greek Old Testament and the more recent Masoretic text in Hebrew agree that it is not the woman herself who wins the victory in this enmity to death, but rather it will be a future male child who is not at all identified as the offspring or seed of Adam but only or uniquely as the offspring of the woman Eve; a very strange and puzzling idea that a woman's seed or offspring is a referent for identity rather than the child's father, not unlike the unusual reference to Jesus as merely: "son of Mary" but not "son of Joseph" by the Evangelists. In fact, "son of Joseph" is not the Evangelists own way of referring to Jesus at all. The custom is perhaps a development from Matthew's indication, where we learned that Mary is a virgin and that the child is from her and the Holy Spirit. This requires Matthew formally to describe only Mary as the mother of the offspring. Let us see the Old Testament paradigm whose prophetic reception refers to the seed of Abraham as fulfilled by Mary's conceiving this same seed from herself alone:

LXX Genesis 3:15:

I will put enmity in **between you and the woman and between your seed and her seed**, **he** *will lie in wait for your head.*

LXX Genesis 17:7:

---

[62] See Brown, *Mary in the New Testament*, 136-137, where his general conclusion (though without all the evidence here provided) affirm such a positive estimate of Mary in Luke's Gospel.

I will establish my covenant as an everlasting covenant **between me and you** [Abraham] **and your seed after you** for the generations to come, *to be your God and of your* **seed** *after you*.

The covenant to refrain from the forbidden fruit, made between Adam and Eve, preserved their immortality and friendship with God. When they decided for disobedience, enmity was created in the world between Eve along with her seed or offspring and Satan.[63] What is more, immortality and hope of a stringent friendship with God was lost, often described as loss of their original justice or grace in God's sight.

The next time that the verse of Genesis 3:15 is repeated happens to be by God again, but in announcing a future restoration of the covenant with not only Abraham (by his faith) but especially with his offspring. This looks very much like, if Eve is ever going to have her offspring vindicate humans before their original accuser Satan, it must happen through the Abrahamic lineage. Abraham has God's promise of a covenant fulfilled to him after meeting "the Angel of Lord" who is mysterious a Trinity of persons, all of whom are called one Lord in Genesis chapter 18. The eternal Word of God, Jesus, had not yet become enfleshed, but he came in the form of one of the three divine Angels of the Lord and he anticipated his own miraculous birth to save God's people. Abraham, as in Rublev's famous icon of the Trinity, has the first historical encounter with the Triune God.[64]

---

[63] The final book of the Bible returns to this enmity between the serpent and "her seed" (*sperma autês*) (Revelation 12:17). Because Revelation refers to the woman bearing the child of promise, the patristic tradition will begin to identify Mary here (we should note that the debate among Greek Christians regarding Revelation's inspired status for centuries likely delayed patristic consideration of Mary in the text). Mary is overshadowed in Revelation by an eagle (whose wings represent Yahweh's theophany; Exodus 19:4). This is a reminiscence of Luke 1:35 and the two overshadowing beings of Son and Spirit that make her the Ark of the Covenant, loosely associated with Mary by allusion in Revelation 11:19.

[64] This is standard interpretation. See for example quotes provided by M. Sheridan (ed.), *Genesis 12–50* (Downers Grove, IL: InterVarsity Press, 2002), 61, 63-64, 66: St. Ephraim the Syrian: "Therefore the Lord, who had just appeared to him at the door of the tent, now appeared to Abraham clearly in one of the three. Abraham then fell down and worshiped him."; St. Ambrose: "Abraham, who was glad to receive strangers, faithful to God and tireless in his service and prompt in fulfilling his duty, saw the Trinity typified.";

Abraham sees three beings, Father, Son, and Spirit. When Abraham saw the Lord (three angels), he fell down prostrate. Like the ceremony of Jesus at the Last Supper –signifying the baptism of the apostles– Abraham washes the feet of the angels, for Jesus was himself baptized, and then washed in turn the feet of his disciples and ate the Last Supper. Finally, Abraham brings the angels three loaves of bread. Jesus will later claim in John's Gospel that Abraham had really met Jesus at Mamre, heard about the ultimate wonder-child to come, "and was glad" (John 8:56). Jesus was quite serious. Recall, Jesus compared the kingdom of heaven to Abraham's wife Sarah who made three loaves (for the Father, Son, and Spirit): "The kingdom of heaven is like yeast that a woman took and mixed in with three measures of flour until all of it was leavened" (Matthew 13:33). Of course, the first verse of Matthew chapter one tell us that a new kingdom comes by Mary's generation of Jesus, which begins and terminates with him for he has no successors! Jesus recounted to Jews his personal ministry and preaching the Gospel of the incarnation or the coming of a more wonderful child than Isaac from Abraham's covenantal seed, destined to win the battle between Eve and Satan. Jesus testified: "'But I do know [the Father] and I keep his word. Your ancestor Abraham rejoiced that he would see my day; he saw it and was glad.' But the Jews said to him, 'You are not yet fifty years old, and have you seen Abraham?'" (John 8:55-57). Jesus recalled his visit to Abraham's tent as the prefigurement or pattern or type of a miracle of his own angelic coming (that is, being sent from the Father) in the flesh as Mary's unique offspring.

Jesus, as we said, spoke about Abraham's wife Sarah who made three loaves (for the Father, Son, and Spirit) at their visit: "The kingdom of heaven is like yeast that a woman took and mixed in with three measures of flour until all of it was leavened." Sarah's annunciation imperfectly prefigured that of Mary. Sarah stood in front of her "tent" at her annunciation. The term "tent" is code for flesh in passages of the Old and New Testament. For instance, the term signals a type of Christ's flesh in the tomb who "pitches a tent [read: "flesh"] in hope" to see God's face (Acts 2:26). Paul asserts that our earthly "tent" (body) passes away but we enter the heavenly tent or "house not-made-by-human-hands" (= dwelling with the body of Jesus) (2 Corinthians 5:1; compare Hebrews 8:2-5, 9:11). Paul, as "tentmaker" (Acts 18:3), prepares people's flesh for glory! When Jesus at the end

---

St. Caesarius of Arles, He received the three men and served them loaves out of three measures. "Why is this, brothers, unless it means the mystery of the Trinity?"

of time shall come, he will be put "on the throne" pitching his tent in the saints (*skênôsei ep'autous*) and will pasture them from the heavenly throne forever (Revelation 7:15-17).

Now, this angelically disguised Father, Son, and Spirit announced a miraculous birth to Sarah at her "tent" or in her "flesh" where she laughs seemingly incredulously. About 2000 years later, the Evangelist Luke records Mary similarly saying the exact opposite. When a created angel –clearly named Gabriel– announces that Jesus "the power of the Most High" and the Holy Spirit will come upon her (Luke 1:35), she –though like Sarah not understanding everything– says piously "So be it (to me according to your word)" or "Amen."

It is highly significant that Sarah's annunciation happens at her tent but that she never joins Abraham to be overshadowed under the oak of Mamre, which shows that Isaac is not the child of promise, who is hinted to have the name (Mr.) "Wonderful." The "overshadowing" and "shade" which become more explicit themes in rest of the Old Testament and become code words for Yahweh's most intensive presence possible. Sarah's laughter leads to her rebuke that signals that the miracle of *Isaac*'s conception will *not* be from "the woman's offspring/seed" (Genesis 3:15) to crush the head of the accuser but Isaac will be only the result from a normal act of marital love.

The Trinity under the shade of the overshadowing oak of Mamre prophetically hints to Sarah: "Why did Sarah laugh, and say, 'Shall I indeed bear a child, now that I am old?' Is anything too wonderful for the Lord?" (Genesis 18:13-14). This is important, for Mary in Luke's Gospel will say oppositely that she is under a life-long vow of virginity (as we shall shortly prove), so how can Mary have a child? Notice: "you shall bear a child," are the very words used by Gabriel to Mary in Luke's Gospel. The Trinitarian prophecy follows, namely, a miracle child is a case of what is merely something wonderful. Isaac is not the most wonderful thing the Lord has in store. We will find out that "too wonderful" is not the name of an event, but of a person; Mr. Wonderful (Judges 13:18)! Here, the Hebrew version of the Old Testament is equally important for us to get the whole picture. Soon, "(Mr.) Wonderful" will be revealed as the literal name of that "Angel of the Lord"! For now, in salvation history, we should note the Sarah stands as a hint, or a foreshadowing, of some more miraculous conception of Abrahamic seed that will make Isaac's situation pale in comparison. Sarah didn't know it, but she served as a pattern to recognize the moment when a perfect person, who will be the woman anticipated by Genesis 3:15, shall conceive personal seed or singular offspring belonging to herself who is named "(Mr.) Wonderful." What would Sarah have experienced, if only she had bothered to step under the overshadowing oak of Mamre with three divine persons? This would presumably have been more like Mary's annunciation, but indeed Sarah lacked the holiness attributed to Mary in Luke's Gospel. It appears that special qualities beyond Sarah were required to be Jesus's biological mother.

The most important connection of the hint of a "(too) wonderful" in the Genesis 18:14 miracle next occurs in the book of Judges chapter 13. We see here the basic elements for God's fulfilling his promise to Abraham. Here, we begin the chapter by noticing that "the Philistines" did evil to Israel for forty years; a propitious prefiguring of Jesus, who afterward will inaugurate a fast of forty days. Lest it just be thought that this is one of many cases of the sacred number forty, we should realize that the divine-like child, Samson, will be born in this chapter: "He who shall begin to deliver Israel from […] the Philistines" (Judges 13:5). Eventually, this phraseology is changed by "save the people from the Philistines" in subsequent Scripture (e.g. 1 Samuel 7:8). Compare this to Matthew 1:21: "She will bear a son, and you are to name him Jesus, for he shall save his people from their sins." Samson is styled to be something like "superman" with powers that seem unbelievable, and this is with good reason. Although Jesus is the invisible and immaterial Word of God united to flesh, Samson is merely human –if barely so– as Samson does Herculean exploits of the flesh (for example, military marvels). This sets up the Old Testament to anticipate that whoever fulfills the type of Samson in the New Testament must be able to do signs and wonders greater than these. The bar is set very high for what kind of marvels this wonderchild must perform. Jesus's more wonderful marvels contrary to laws of nature do surpass Samson, but it is his moral perfection in contrast to Samson's martial prowess that will signal a prophetic shift of focus in the upcoming prophecy of the virgin birth (Isaiah 9:6). Jesus's coming will save us principally from spiritual, not entirely from our political, maladies. A stable political order is not guaranteed eternally on the earth only holiness. In this, Jesus can be a blessing for all nations, since the one thing shared between many cultures, languages, and peoples is the divinely wrought soul or rationality of humans, which needs deliverance from unruly thoughts and passions.

The Angel of the Lord named "(Mr.) Wonderful" (viz., pre-Incarnate Jesus) tells Samson's Father, Manoah, something that will serve as the pattern for

Samsonite-Nazirites in the future (Judges 13:15): (1.) The mother makes a vow (she must promise never –as a Nazirite female– to drink wine or grape), (2.) The Nazarite male shall belong to the Lord as *one holy from the womb* (Judges 13:7), and (3.) There is associated with such Nazirites an offering, whether symbolic or a burnt offering (Hebrew: *hōlâh*) as part of a ritual (Judge 13:16). Strangely, however, an Angel of the Lord or Yahweh in the guise of a man revealing his secret name as "(Mr.) Wonderful" to Manoah (when pressed to say who he really is) who sacrifices himself in the fire set by Manoah. No explicit mention in Judges chapter 13 is made of the customary sacrifice for Samson, as if the Angel of the Lord is himself the original holocaust unto himself! This pattern of a vow, sacrifice after a miracle, and child-turned-Nazirite from the womb recurs again with Hanna and Samuel:

> Hannah stood up. Now Eli the priest was sitting on his chair by the doorpost of the Lord's house. In her deep anguish Hannah prayed to the Lord, weeping bitterly. (1.) And she made a vow, saying, "Lord Almighty, if you will only look on your servant's lowliness-sterility and remember me, and not forget your servant but give her a son, then (3.) I will give him to the Lord for all the days of his life, (2.) and no razor will ever be used on his head." (1 Samuel 1:9-11)

Ultimately, Mary's future annunciation and nativity follow this pattern in Luke chapter 1. Originally, Samson's mom needed to become a female **Nazir**ite (Greek: *Naziraios*) *before she was worthy of bearing a godlike child of promise to deliver Israel*. Of course, Samson's type of Nazirite vow means only that the male never cuts his hair. In Samson's special case (chosen to be a special kind of Nazirite from the womb), there is no termination to the vow, by either Samson or his mom.

As we have already explored, Matthew 2:23 reads: "He shall be called a **Naz(i)r**ene (Greek: *Nazoraios*)"; this is meant to play on this Old Samsonite-**Nazir**ite prophecy fulfilled by Jesus a Samsonite-Nazarite. This explains why Jesus is always depicted with unshorn hair. In her own time, Mary speaks to Gabriel the same phrases of past women Nazarites; namely, the Mother of Samson and Hannah (mother of the prophet Samuel). But Matthew hints that Jesus is born

74

in "**Naza**reth"[65] (compare LXX Judges 13:5, 7: "*Naziraios*"), while Samson is established immediately by God as "a **Nazi**rite from his mother womb." Like Abraham-Sarah-Isaac, Manoah-the mother of Samson only imperfectly hint at the future perfection in Yahweh-Mary-Jesus. So, Israel must await the perfect deliverer. Jesus of **Naza**reth signals the divine comedy by which both a Samsonite Nazirite (only required not to cut his hair) is dedicated to God from the womb, but who also is symbolized as both successor and bloodline of David by his birth in Bethlehem. His early-womb and childhood period are spent in Nazareth, while his birthday is in Bethlehem –Jesus is dedicated in utero to God just like Samson and Samuel. This will come into play in Luke 2:22, where the Mosaic Law supposes a male firstborn to be dedicated to God from the womb. Jesus fulfills the Egyptian-Passover, Nazarite, and Mosaic shadows at his purification with Mary as unusually described by Luke, which we shall see in chapter 4.

If Genesis 3:15, or the "seed of woman," will one day deliver God's people from Adam's sin. God has only selected the male "seed of Abraham" so far in the Abraham-Isaac-Jacob, Samson, and even Samuel histories. The mention of "too wonderful" in comparison Sarah's child in Genesis 18:14 is supplemented by "(Mr.) Wonderful" revealing himself as the Angel of the Lord who is present at Samson's miraculous conception so far. Hannah is another case of this, but Mary's Annunciation and birth of him who is called "Wonderful" is quite exceptional. "(Mr.) Wonderful," vaguely revealed to be one of the angelic Trinity at the oak of Mamre, is the same "Wonderful" producing Samson by miracle and now inside the womb of a virgin.

Eventually, we do see the verbiage of Genesis 3:15 pop up one more time in the history of the seed of Abraham. The prophetic moment happens to assure the Israelites that the house of David or the patrilineal descent of David's seed is the legitimate family from whom we await the wonderchild to save Israel and to be a blessing for all nations. Let us take a look at 1 Samuel 20:41-42:

> After the boy had gone, David got up from the south side of the
> stone and bowed down before Jonathan three times, with his face
> to the ground. Then they kissed each other and wept together—

---

[65] From the verb נזר (*nazar*), to consecrate oneself; Nazareth (given the Galilean pronunciation) would indicate "consecrating" and "*nazir*" is the one consecrated from the womb.

but David wept the most. Jonathan said to David, "Go in peace, for we have sworn friendship with each other in the name of the Lord, saying, '*The Lord is witness between you and me, and between your seed and my seed forever.*'" Then David left, and Jonathan went back to the town.

The Trinitarian peace agreement between the two invokes the Abraham's Trinitarian Lord to recognize a covenant of peace between the bloodline of the first and second kingly lines of Yahweh's people. Failure of David to connect himself as a true successor to Saul's and Jonathan's divinely elected kingship means that he cannot be a "christ" or an anointed one by Yahweh as the proper ruler over God's people. If Mary is a virgin from this line, then she will be the woman to have her own seed to complete the Genesis 3:15 prophecy and, therefore, Jesus can be called "son of Mary" alone and the Jewish custom of calling a child by its father's name can be omitted completely as the Evangelists are wont to do often.

From this line of David, who has connected his seed to Genesis 3:15 by replacing the line of Saul, there comes one more prefiguring annunciation to the line of King David before the beginning of the political destruction of Israel beginning around 700 BC. The seed of Abraham was being constantly accompanied by Yahweh in its political history. However, even in great prosperity, there was great sin that displeased God. So, the Lord provided for the political destruction of the kingdom in consequence of sin. This suggested that sin was the real culprit, not poor practice of political science. Consequently, the prophet Isaiah spoke of the politically weak but spiritually strong Davidic King, Hezekiah, as prefiguring the coming of the "wonderful" child to redeem and save God's people: Yahweh himself shall give a sign: "Behold the virgin will receive and conceive in her womb a son, and you shall call his name Immanuel" (LXX Isaiah 7:14). We saw in chapter 1 that Isaiah's phraseology is taken from two separate passages of Scripture (Genesis 16:11; Judges 13:5). The child predicted to King Hezekiah will somehow be like Hagar (exiled to Egypt with her son who is cast out of his proper house though Ishmael is of the one seed of Abraham), but the child will additionally be like Samson, dedicated from the womb and called "son of God" (Hebrew = *ben Elohim*). So, if the child is a new Samson or godlike figure and son of God, it is no surprise that he will be able to counter the true enemy besieging Israel (sin and death) and the child will also be called by Isaiah: "God is with us." All the annunciations in the past were to old women who were sterile: Sarah, Samson's mom, and Hannah. But the Hebrew version or Masoretic text of Isaiah

7:14 emphasizes a paradigm shift: No longer will a marvelous pregnancy beyond nature take place with sterile widows but with something even more unthinkable: a young unmarried maiden (*almah*). Naturally, the significance of this prophecy was elaborated perhaps a hundred and fifty or so years before the birth of Christ by translating "young unmarried maiden" as the equivalent in Greek to "virgin." Isaiah added a new attribute onto this upcoming miraculous annunciation, namely, that she never knows (intimately) a man and yet conceives a child.

In Isaiah's prophecy we see entirely familiar elements, namely, (1.) a miraculous shadow moving as miraculous proof to Hezekiah (similar to Mamre and to the Ark of the Covenant's overshadowing by angel wings) and (2.) a "Wonderful" person named to be born from this unmarried young maiden without the intervention of male seed. What is more, by use of both the Hebrew and Greek Bibles, we notice that they equally attest to the child of promise to being named "(Mr.) Wonderful" of Judges 13:18. The Septuagint (LXX) calls the child born of a virgin (Isaiah 7:14), "the Angel of Great Counsel" (LXX Isaiah 9:6) who gave advice to Manoah, while the Hebrew calls him by his name revealed to Manoah: "Wonderful." Both of them point back to the place where an Angel = Wonderful, namely, the Angel at the annunciation to Samson's mom, and "(Mr.) Wonderful's" counsel given to Manoah and his wife.

> His name is called "Angel of Great Counsel" [Hebrew: "Wonderful"] for I will bring peace upon the rulers [. . .] His government will be great and of his peace there will be no end: upon the throne of David to establish it kingdom with judgment and with righteousness, from henceforth and forever. (LXX Isaiah 9:6–7)

No longer is there a hint of something "too wonderful" according to the Angel of the Lord to Sarah in Genesis 18:14, no longer does the Angel who counsels Manoah, named "(too) Wonderful" stand outside of a womb blessing a wonderchild, but now the Angel (Mr.) Wonderful is inside of a womb or incarnate, the pre-Incarnate Jesus is predicted to come into a young maiden's womb. The chain of prophecy links Old Testament and the New Testament: "Behold, a virgin (*parthenos*) will have and will conceive a son and you will call his name Emmanuel (God-with-us)" (LXX Isaiah 7:14). This phrase is linked among the following: (1) (Mr.) Wonderful's self-revelation to Manoah, (2.) Isaiah's prediction of (Mr.) Wonderful's becoming incarnate and being born, (3.) Mary's birthing Jesus. Augustine provides an enlightening summation of the Christian tradition on this point:

> Earlier times were granted the prophets inspired and filled with the Word of God; we have been granted the Word of God himself as the prophet. But Christ, the Lord of the prophets, [is] a prophet in the same way as Christ, the Lord of angels, [is] an angel. For he himself also was called an "Angel of Great Counsel." But even so, what does the prophet say elsewhere? That not as a legate nor as an angel, but he himself, coming, will save them, that is, for saving them he will not send a legate, he will not send an angel, but he himself will come. Who will come? The Angel himself.[66]

Now we see the link: Sarah's less-than-too-wonderful Isaac is not the child of promise, nor Samson whom Mr. Wonderful miraculously brings into existence, but rather the Angel-Wonderful or pre-Incarnate Jesus become God-with-us in a virgin's womb. At the moment of Mary's birthing, we come full circle for the angel Gabriel says of Mary's conception (using Genesis 18:14 verbatim): "For nothing is impossible/too wonderful for God" (compare Luke 1:37).[67] Here it is! The child is conceived by Mary, Gabriel immediately announced it to be "too Wonderful," as mentioned first in Genesis 18:14, then in Judges 13, then in Isaiah 9:6 – from the line of Abraham and Isaac! But *how does Scripture prove by Scripture that only a perpetual virgin shall bear the wonderchild?*

---

[66] Augustine of Hippo, *Tractates on the Gospel of John 11-27*, ed. T.P. Halton, trans. J.W.Rettig, Fathers of the Church (Washington DC: CUA Press, 1988), 79:38.

[67] Tertullian knew the force of this argument, even used by competing Christian sects, in the late-second and early-third centuries. See Tertullian, *Against Praxeas*, ed. A. Roberts, J. Donaldson, and A. C. Coxe, trans. P. Holmes, *Latin Christianity: Its Founder, Tertullian* (Buffalo, NY: Christian Literature Company, 1885), 3:605: "Therefore, they argue, it was not difficult for God to make Himself both a Father and a Son, contrary to the condition of things among men. For a barren woman to have a child against nature was no difficulty with God; nor was it for a virgin to conceive. Of course nothing is 'too hard [wonderful] for the Lord.'"

2.5 Mary: Perpetual Virgin Mother of the Wonderchild

Luke is a master storyteller. If we look at Luke chapter 1 from the perspective of his quotes that are meant to put meat on the bones of his claims of both typology and prophecy fulfillment, then we find Luke's story of Mary, the virgin birth, and Mary's perpetual virginity in about five tiers of texts from prior prophecy and Old Testament Scripture:

(1.) Tier one for the virgin birth is adapted from Genesis: Abraham and Sarah's annunciations

(2.) Tier two for the virgin birth is adapted from Samson's mother's annunciation

(3.) Tier three for perpetual virginity is adapted from Jephthah's vow of his daughter to perpetual virginity by the Holy Spirit

(4.) Tier four for the virgin birth is adapted from Hannah's annunciation

(5.) Tier five for the virgin's purity is adapted from the Ark of the Covenant in 1 Samuel

Let's compare Luke to his literary sources. This will tell us exactly how Luke's storytelling has increased in its complexity over Matthew and Mark:

In the sixth month, in the first day of the month, the word of the Lord by Haggai the prophet came unto Zerubbabel the son of Shealtiel, governor of Judah, and to Joshua the son of Josedech, the high priest.[68] (LXX Haggai 1:1)

An angel [Gabriel] **was sent** in power **from heaven** and announced **and said** (LXX Daniel 4:13):

---

[68] Matthew 1:12 agrees with 1 Chronicles 3:19, namely, Zerubbabel is son of Shealtiel (the line of Jesus of Nazareth). This is typically contrasted to Luke 3:27-28, where David's line of Nathan is connected to an unknown Neri said to be Sheltiel's Father leading to Jesus of Nazareth. However, Luke 1:26 suggests a typological-genealogical connection between Jesus's namesake, the great high priest, and the line of Zerubbabel-Shealtiel.

David *did not wish to move* the Ark of the Lord's Covenant *into the city* ^{of David} and David sequestered (*apekleinon*) it in the house of Obededom of _{Goetha} (*Geththaiou*) for three months ([LXX=] 2 Samuel 6:10)

<u>In the sixth month,</u> **Gabriel the angel was sent from God** *to Nazareth, in a city of* _{Galilee} [...] *to a man whose name was Joseph, of* ^{the house of David} (Luke 1:26-27)

Luke cites Old Testament modes of expression; even the phrase about the sixth month uniquely reflects the word of the Lord coming to the prophet Haggai and a high priest named Jesus. Expanding the work on Mary by Rev. Dr. Brown, we next see Luke's dependence on texts from the prophet Daniel and (even more fully than Brown investigates) 2 Samuel 6. So, the Gabriel of the end times, the last of the prophetical books before the prophet St. John the Forerunner of Jesus, comes to Nazareth since –like David awaiting the return of the disappeared Ark– a fit dwelling in "David's city" must be prepared for it. The *Protevangelium* in the first or second century also underlines that in the background is Mary the New Ark whose doors (or privy members) are shut up until she, as Ark, can be brought to Jerusalem. As Mary is shut up in the *Protevangelium* by Joseph, so nobody can touch her (including Joseph who is absent); so, too, is the Ark beyond the reach of any human. While Mary awaits her entrance into "David's city" in _{Galilee} (*Galilaios*) the olden Ark awaited its entrance in the house of Obededom of _{Goetha} (*Geththaios*). The wordplay is obvious. And, as we shall see, Mary shall imitate the sequestration of the Ark during her pregnancy by going to her cousins' house "for three months" (see Luke 1:56). It is fascinating, upon learning of the blessing that the Ark brings to Obededom's house outside of "David's city," David then want to carry the Ark to his own town: "So David went and brought up the Ark of God from the house of Obededom to the City of David with gladness" (2 Samuel 6:12).[69]

For now, we skip over Mary's designation as "full of grace" (Luke 1:28-29) and go immediately to the verses that prepare us to understand Mary's perpetual virginity in imitation of the purity and freedom from the touch of man that is due to the Ark of the Covenant. Luke 1:28-29 hearken to Sirach 18:17, and the major and minor prophets, but the announcement that Mary is "highly favored" or "full of grace" has no direct bearing on her virgin birth and subsequent perpetual virginity. But we shall address this in the next chapter. Also, Luke 1:30, 38, and

---

[69] Ark typology has long ago been catalogued. For the most recent summary of the Biblical arguments, see Laurentin, *Présence de Marie*, 22-25.

its discussion of grace and Mary's being a slave of the Lord refer to the words of the prophetess Hannah to interpret Luke's meaning. We shall address these in the next chapter as well. Luke 1:31 addresses the prophecy of the virgin birth and it is here that we pick back up and, to an extent, review what we already saw from chapter 1 regarding the Samson as a type of Jesus:

"And behold you will have in your womb and bear a son (*idou su en gastri hekseis kai teksêi huion*)" […] The woman conceived and bore a son and called his name Samson (*eteken hê gynê huion kai ekalesen to onoma autou Sampson*)" (Judges 13:6, 24)[70]

"And behold you will conceive in your womb and bear a son and will call his name Jesus (*kai idou syllêmpsêi en gastri kai teksêi huion*)"[71] (Luke 1:31)

Like Samson's mom, Mary will miraculously bear as a Nazirite son and call him Jesus, for he will "save their people from Philistines/sins." Jesus who is (Mr.) Wonderful appeared personally, as recounted within the Book of Judges, in the form of the Angel of Great Counsel ("Wonderful"), which as we saw in chapter 1 is the very source for part of Isaiah's prophecy identifying the wonderchild or God-with-Us (Emmanuel), whose name is the same as the Angel of the Lord in Judges chapter 13 and whose titles are like Samson who is called "son of God." All of a sudden, after such concentration on the Angel of Great Counsel or "Wonderful" who was both at the annunciation of Samson and the replacement for Samson's sacrifice to the Lord later in the chapter, Luke surprisingly and abruptly jumps to citing Judges chapter 11 to borrow yet more phraseology in order to describe Mary. Why?

Unexpectedly, Luke seems to want to go a step farther than Matthew's infancy narrative. If Matthew sought to demonstrate that Mary had only one child, that she conceived and bore that child as a virgin, and that Joseph was unaccustomed to have relations with her though they lived together in both Bethlehem and Nazareth, it still requires us to go a step farther and simply declare

---

[70] Compare also: "And she bore a son and called his name Samuel (*kai eteken huion kai ekalesen to onoma autou Samouêl*)" ([LXX=] 1Samuel 1:20).

[71] Compare: "Behold the Virgin shall possess in her womb and bear a son (*Idou hê Parthenos en gastri heksei kai teksetai huion*)" (Matthew 1:23).

that Mary was perpetually a virgin. After all, to conceive only one child is perhaps a sign of poor fertility on the man or woman's part. To say that Joseph continuously did not know Mary suggests only that Joseph and Mary never had relations, but it does not mean that Mary could not have married a second husband and had children, if she had wanted. Of course, everyone agrees that the Bible cannot be read to suppose Mary was ever married a second time, but the question is whether she *might have married and had relations*, even if Joseph and she refrained from relations (which is itself a very odd scenario for supposing among Jews of the first century). At any rate, to dispel every doubt about both the virgin birth and about Adam's and Abraham's family culminating and terminating in the eternal king or offspring Jesus, Luke borrowed from the only example of a female practicing virginity in the Old Testament. Let us see the verbal parallels between Judges and Luke below:

Judges chapter 11:29-31, 34, 37-39:

Luke chapter 1:34-5, 37-389, 41-42, 56:

The Lord's spirit was born *upon Jephthah* (egenêthê epi Iephthae pneuma kyriou)[72] […] and he made a vow to the Lord: "If you give the Ammonites into my hands, whatever comes out of the door of my house to meet me when I return in triumph from the Ammonites will be the Lord's, and I will sacrifice it as a holocaust" […] Jephthah returned to his house […] And [the dedicated virgin] said to her Father: And do to me this your word (poiêson moi to rhêma)

And Mary said to the angel [Gabriel]: "In what way shall this be, since **I know not man** (andra ou ginôsko;) [35]and the angel answered her: "The Holy *Spirit will come upon you* (pneuma hagion epeleusetai epi se) […] and the one born (gennômenon) shall be called holy […] "No discourse shall be 'too wonderful/impossible' from God." […] And Mary said: · "May it happen to me according to your word (genoito moi kat to rhêma sou)" […] Then did arise Mary in those days AND WENT (eporeuthê) to the mountain country

---

[72] See Justin Martyr, *Dialogue avec Trypon: Édition critique, traduction, commentaire*, ed. Phillip Bobichon, Paradosis 47 (Fribourg: University of Fribourg, 2003), 1:454 (chapter 100.5): "Gabriel the angel evangelized her that: 'The Lord's spirit (*pneuma kyriou*) shall come (*epi*) upon you […] for the one born (*gennômenon*) from her is holy.'" Justin adapts Luke 1:35 to coincide with Judges 11:28 as his model, betraying either confusion or mental cross-referencing between the two. This might account for patristic arguments linking Luke 1:34 to perpetual virginity (Judges 11:39), though fourth-century Fathers do not detail the origin of their tradition.

[Jephthah] said: "go (*poreuou*)" and he sent her out for two months; SHE WENT (*eporeuthê*) too UNTO HER NEIGHBORS and they wept over her [perpetual] virginity (*ta parthenia autês*) [73] on the mountains. **She knew not man** (*autê ouk egnô andra*).[74]

with haste unto the city of Juda AND SHE ENTERED INTO THE HOUSE OF ZACHARIAH AND GREETED ELIZABETH. And it happened as Elizabeth heard the greeting [...] [41]ELIZABETH WAS FILLED WITH THE HOLY SPIRIT. And Elizabeth cried aloud and said "Blessed are you among women and blessed the fruit of your womb [...] Mary remained with her up to three months and then returned into her house.

First of all, Judges chapter 11 is the story of Jephthah. The story goes as follows: (1.) Jephthah was inspired by the "The Lord's spirit" the same "Holy Spirit" that came upon Mary in Luke 1:35 above. (2.) Jephthah is even said to have this Spirit born upon him just like Mary who bore Christ by the Spirit. This Lord's spirit causes Jephthah to make a vow, very much like Mary (in the image of Samson's mother and Hannah) who presumptively vows since like Hannah Mary finds "grace before the Lord" (1 Samuel 1:18). Jephthah, under influence of the Spirit vows to dedicate the first being that he will run into, if he should crush the polytheist or incestuous-children of Lot by a great victory. Who does Yahweh providentially make him run into? Well, he encounters his "only begotten daughter" who is nameless but whom he loves above all. Biblical scholars have several theories about what Jephthah's vow meant. Jephthah vowed his daughter's:[75] (1.) virginity until death by human sacrifice, (2.) her perpetual

---

[73] The Masoretic is clear: *bǝṯūlay* (virginity) that is lamentably perpetual as the result of her Father's vow to God.

[74] This is in direct contrast to the natural physically natural conception of Anna: "And he knew his wife Anna (*kai egnô tên Annan gynaika autou*)" (1sam1:19). In fact, this is opposite of all great conceptions (e.g., the same phrase in Genesis 4 for the conception of Adam by Eve, et al.).

[75] See Bernard Robinson, "The Story of Jephthah and His Daughter: Then and Now," *Biblica* 85 (2004): 331-348, especially 345-346. The author has traced the typological reading of the virgin-sacrifice back to three lines: (1.) A third-century tradition witnessed by Aphraat that see the flesh of the daughter as anticipating the fleshly virginal sacrifice of Jesus, (2.) A Palestinian tradition of the seventh century, in an artistic panel, where Jephthah offers the virginal flesh as if Christ. Both of these are concentrated on the flesh of Jesus, (3.) A Latin tradition beginning with the Venerable Bede (?). Once

virginity but without human sacrifice (3.) her perpetual virginity and offering an animal-substitutionary sacrifice, (4.) his daughter's perpetual virginity as the holocaust or sacrifice.[76] Jephthah is principally worried about his daughter's virginity that will prevent her from producing Abraham's seed and perpetuating the promise of Genesis 18:14, but God inspired paradoxically that he forcibly vow his only begotten daughter to perpetual virginity (a singular case in the Old Testament)! Let us read the passage in its own right:

> When Jephthah returned to his home [...] who should come out to meet him but his daughter, dancing to the sound of timbrels! She was an only child. [...] When he saw her, he [...] cried, "Oh no, my daughter! You have brought me down and I am devastated. I have made a vow to the Lord that I cannot break." "My father," she replied, "you have given your word to the Lord. do to me this your word, [...] But grant me this one request," she said. "Give me two months to roam the mountains and weep with my friends, because of my virginity." "You may go," he said. And he let her go for two months. She and her friends went into the hills and wept her virginity. After the two months, she returned to his house, and he did to her as he had vowed. **And she did not know man**. (Judges 11:34-39)

The situation is stunning, for Luke's annunciation has Gabriel, as the Lord's representative, play the part of Jephthah and Mary quotes verbatim Jephthah's ever-virgin daughter by responding enthusiastically to the plan of perpetual virginity entailed by the votive sacrifice as inspired by the Holy Spirit. Finally, notice that the sundry words of Judges are that the perpetual virgin dwells in a house but nothing more. Of course, this is only too convenient for Luke to emphasize Mary dwelling in Joseph's house as a virgin. Mary, however, shall be pregnant, although a virgin! So, naturally Mary adds a phrase lacking to Jephthah's

---

Mariological reflections burgeon (post-431), it is unsurprising that tradition begins underlining that Jesus's only biological donor is Mary and, thus, his fleshly sacrifice is of Mary's flesh, which by extension must be virginal.

[76] For the various theories, see David Marcus, *Jepthah and His Vow* (Lubbock: Texas Tech Press, 1986), 26.

ever-virgin daughter: "How shall this be, because **I do not know man**."[77] Here, Luke infallibly emphasizes Mary's vow to perpetual virginity. As the result of Gabriel's influence and the Holy Spirit's miracle-making pregnancy, Mary has been vowed and sacrificed as a perpetual virgin! Mary substantially asserts in Luke the following: "How can a future be where I will be pregnant with a child, because **I am the new only-begotten daughter of Jephthah, a perpetually consecrated virgin, bound to die in virginity**?"[78] Luke quotes from Judges 11:39 the only other such phrase in the entire history of the Greek language. It can only signify a divinely-predestined perpetual virginity by inspired vow required by the Father of her house under inspiration of the Holy Spirit. There can be no doubt what Luke conveys by an exact quote of Judges. Luke's typology betrays why God recorded in the Old Testament this potentially disagreeable or even scandalous sacrifice of Jephthah in the first place, namely, as an anticipation of Mary's fulfillment of a productive virginity *without perpetual mourning.*

Instead of Mary *bemoaning* her virginity for two months as a perpetual curse, she goes to the mountains to where her neighbors and cousins, Zachariah and Elizabeth *celebrate* her perpetual virginity as the very means by which God – contrary to all expectation– blesses Israel with a wonderchild. Perpetual virginity, once considered a perpetual curse for blocking production of the seed of promise,

---

[77] See Brown, *The Birth of the Messiah*, 289, where he emphasizes that this: "because," is causal. So, we expect that: "I do not man" is somehow causal of prevention of conception in the contingent future.

[78] See, for example, an author (1130–1203), Martin Legionensis, *Sermon 30: On the Ascension of Christ* (*Patrologia Latina* 208:1144D):

> The virgin daughter of the Judge Jephthah certainly prefigured by way
> of type (*typice praefiguravit*) this virginal flesh of Jesus Christ, taken
> from the virgin mother and the offered [flesh] in the odor of sweetness,
> when her same father returned as victor from war; he offered it to God.

This insight is given as the type and rationale in Medieval books for the feast of the Mary's Entry into the temple where her virginity is offered by her parents to God. See Manuscript, *Harley 2838*, f. 8r (quotes Judges 11:39 in the medieval book: *Speculum humanae salvationis*).

is no longer the curse of Jephthah but the very blessing of Israel![79] Instead of bewailing perpetual virginity every year among the kinsmen of Jephthah, Elizabeth, Mary's kinswoman cries out: "Blessed are you among women!" (Luke 1:28) and Mary notes that all generation will call her blessed! This is quite a reversal of the lot of perpetual virginity. Luke seems to opt from among legitimate scholarly interpretations of Jephthah's sacrifice in Judges chapter 11, so that Jephthah's vow was inspired by Yahweh's Spirit as a sort of dedication of virginity to Yahweh. Now this same type is changed into a miraculous birth and the value of perpetual virginity is thereby transformed so that the Nazarites Mary and Jesus are no longer committed, respectively, to not drinking fruit of the vine and not cutting his hair, but to perpetual virginity as the end term of "the promise made to Abraham and his seed forever" (Luke 1:55). The reason, however, for celebration is that virginity, like the lesser marvel of sterility in old age, has also been transformed into something productive of the child of promise. What is beyond dispute is the fact that perpetual virginity is at the center of Mary's response to Gabriel and there is a solution, which is not future sexual activity but a miracle of virgin birth!

Conclusions

In Luke 7:44, the Evangelist explicitly endorsed typology (compare Romans 5:14; 1 Corinthian 10:6, 11; 1 Peter 3:19-21) as God's plan for anticipating the events of the New Testament in the Old Testament. In line with this reading, Mary had also been interpreted in retrospect by Paul according to typology which he had embraced so that Mary conceived by reference only to her womanhood without the intervention of male seed; due to the Protoevangelium (Genesis 3:15). Even Abraham had learned in Genesis chapter 18 that there is a child of promise associated with the name of "too wonderful." Paul saw this typology in child production clearly in Galatians. In the Old Testament, the identity of the one called wonderful becomes gradually clearer by (Mr.) "Wonderful's" self-revelation to a duo of Nazirites, to Mother and her son, Samson. The Nazirite child is always

---

[79] "Three months" (instead "after two months") are in Luke due to the Ark of the Covenant remaining with Obededom's house for three months. The reconciliation is easy enough: The bewailing of virginity is for two months, then the daughter returns and is sacrificed in the third month. The Ark remains without movement for three months in its place. So, Mary is traveling to celebrate (not bewail) her virginity through Elizabeth's inspiration.

associated with a sacrifice and Judges chapter 11 strangely seems to follow this very pattern but without indicating anyone to be a Nazirite. Still, there is a person who has been dedicated (though not from the time of her mother's womb) and who is to be offered or made holy to God by means of a vow. The relationship between Samuel's dedication by Hannah in 1 Samuel chapters 1-2 and the sacrifice of the daughter of Jephthah in Judges chapter 11 have often been linked by modern scholarship. Like modern scholars, Luke sees the Nazirite paradigms of dedication and sacrifice somehow linked to the oddity of perpetual virginity. Mary and Jesus are styled a new type of Nazirite, even if not only this, in order to throw light on the meaning of an Old Testament event; Mary quotes verbatim her predecessor, the daughter of Jephthah, to protest her vow of perpetual virginity to the Angel Gabriel that should impede her conception of any child. Instead of dissuading her from virginity until death, like his own type, Gabriel assures her that divine intervention can leave her vow intact and still produce offspring that will be both the seed of Abraham and "the name" of Yahweh who is called "Wonderful." The ancient tradition of the Christian church –since St. Gregory Nyssa (who wrote in AD 386),[80] St. Ambrose of Milan, and St. Augustine of Hippo– constantly alluded to a tradition of Mary taking a solemn vow at Luke 1:34. However, because they neither betrayed their sources for this tradition, nor their textual basis for such an argument, it was only later in the Middle Ages that other authors found Judges 11:39 to justify the patristic tradition of Mary's virginity. Unfortunately, this historical development has often been understudied by modern scholars of the Bible.

---

[80] See Gregory Nyssa, *Oratio in diem natalem Christi*, Die Weihnachtspredigt Gregors von Nyssa: Überlieferungsgeschichte und Text (Münster: PhD Diss., 1975), 1140D-1140A.

Chapter Three:

Mary in the Gospel of Luke Chapter 1 (Continued)

3.1 The Annunciation and the Doctrine of Grace in Luke 1:26-29

So far, Luke has exponentially increased our theological interest in Mary, from her role in Christ's ministry to aspects of her miraculous conception and ethical life of purity. Let us investigate Luke's verses composed about Mary chronologically. Luke's retelling of Mary's story from a common pool of documents and ostensibly her own eyewitness is of course mentioned at the beginning of the Lucan Gospel:

Old Testament Type:	New Testament Fulfillment:
LXX Haggai 1:1: In the sixth month, the Lord of the Lord to priest Jesus	Luke 1:26: In the sixth month
LXX Daniel 4:13: Angel [Gabriel] from heaven	Luke 1:26: Angel Gabriel from God
2 Samuel 6:10-12: Ark goes to city of David	Luke 1:26-28: Mary goes to Bethlehem to the house of David
LXX Zachariah 9:9; Zephaniah 3:14; Joel 2:21-22: *Chaīre* or summation of joyful message of salvation to mother Zion by the prophets	Luke 1:28: Hail (*Chaīre*) or joyful message of salvation to mother of Savior as fulfilling prophets

LXX Sirach 18:17: The man full of grace (*kecharitômenôi*) brings both a word and a gift

Luke 1:28: The woman of grace (*kecharitômenê*)[81] has long possessed a good word and gift from God

LXX Genesis 15:1-2: The word of the Lord comes to Abram in an annunciation saying: "Don't fear" in a "greeting" because his "merit" is great (*Mê phobou* […] *egô hyperaspizô sou ho misthos sou polus estai sphodra*). He is given a child of promise due to being considered in a state of justice with God by his faith (*episteusen Abram tôi Theôi kai elogisthê autôi eis dikaiosunên*)

Luke 1:28-29: Gabriel's greeting and vocabulary are the same: "greeting" matches uniquely Abram's annunciation by Angel of the Lord. Abram learns that he is just or meritorious in God's sight by faith and has great merit unto a child of promise. So, too, is Mary but she had already been declared "full of grace" prior to her act of faith (*fiat*) upon Gabriel's good news.

LXX Deuteronomy 37:7: Moses is told "the Lord is with you" and puts the law written in a book inside the Ark.

Luke 1:30 Mary is the New Ark of the New Law and the Lord is with her like Moses.

(LXX=) 1 Samuel 1:18: Hannah said: **"your slave has found grace before** your eyes (*euren hê doulê sou charin en ophthamois sou*)"

Don't fear (*Mê phobou*),[82] Mary, for **you have found grace before** God (*eures gar charin para tôi Theôi*)[83]

---

[81] See Raymond Brown, *The birth of the Messiah: A Commentary on the Infancy Narratives in the Gospels of Matthew and Luke*, 2nd ed. (New York; London: Yale University Press, 1993), 288, where he emphasizes the selection of Hannah as a paradigm may have to do with the fact that her name means: "grace," in Hebrew.

[82] This is Mary greeted as the New Abraham (not the disobedient Sarah), for the Angel of the Lord both "greets" (*aspazetai*) and then says "don't fear" to Abraham, just as to Mary.

[83] See Brown, *The Birth of the Messiah*, 289, for the Semiticism underlining Noah's status before God (Genesis 6:9).

Luke, a skilled writer, clearly sees the Greek, Septuagint Scripture as his major inspiration for his choice of storytelling. We can imagine that instead of relying on very literal and clumsy translations of the Aramaic or local language in which many records of Jesus's life and sayings were plausibly collected, Luke chose to render them in a more elegant and respectable Greek. While the Septuagint is not reflective of the virtues of pagan literary writers, it was the oldest document in Greek to render God's revelation intelligible to first-century readers. Hence, we see Luke lifting phrases and vocabulary from the presumably inspired writings of Scripture in preference to any foreign language translations from his originally Semitic documents and witnesses.

Reference to the Angel Gabriel is perfectly poised to bridge the gap between the last prophetic text recorded in the Book of Daniel and the newly revealed Gospel. Luke's constant citations from the Septuagint secure our belief that his: "Hail [Mary]," which is a common greeting is meant for us to refer to the rare times it is used in the Greek Old Testament.[84] There, it is a greeting to daughter Zion, or the Lord's city with its Temple, from which forgiveness of sins is obtained. The fact that there was a first and second Temple and that these had been polluted in the past is quite significant since the reentry of God's Ark to this third Temple (Jesus's flesh), suggests that Mary, as an image of Zion, Jerusalem, and faithful remnant Judah shall maintain the purity that was lost in the history of the prior Temples. Mary is hailed New Zion or the New Temple from which the body of Jesus –whose virginal and Marian flesh will be destroyed and rebuilt in three days– who is soon to be produced. She is the supplier of the igneous material to become unhewn stone or stone rejected by the builders that will be the cornerstone of the New Temple, the third and last Temple of sacrifice to God. Mary, per Luke's sources, plays the New Abraham, the elder of whom had enjoyed a very first annunciation of a wonderchild. The verbal dependence is secured by both the

---

[84] Compare Brown, *Mary in the New Testament*, 128-132. Brown is quite right to deny any obvious allusion to the prophets. I argue, aware of Brown's sound perspicacity, that it is Luke's demonstrable dependence in other verses (some of which have already been admitted and studied by Brown), that parsimony requires us to conclude that: "*Chaire*," is not an exception to the literary form common to all of Luke 1. Luke rearranges preexisting material in an authoritative source (LXX) in order to create a narrative that admittedly includes prophecy fulfillment (e.g., Brown's argument for the virgin birth). Within this context, this entirely common greeting is chosen likewise to strengthen or sustain the overall apologetic and prophetic thrust of Luke chapter 1.

Septuagint's and Luke's combination of terms for an annunciation. We should remember that modern electronic means permit us to assert with security these verbal dependencies in computer search engines and analytical programs that were formerly impossible only several decades ago. Of course, St. Paul had already made the point by Luke's time that Abraham was made a just man (with the virtue of justice) –sometimes called justified or someone enjoying justification– by his faith that came with a divine reward: to bear a child that would be a blessing for the world until the end of time. For Luke, to equate the greeting of Gabriel to the word of God to Abram simply brings us full circle: The child of prophecy has finally come upon us in Mary who must be likewise replete with justice and pleases God.

Mary, at the beginning of her story within the history of salvation, receives Abraham's original "greeting" and phrase: "don't fear." Like Hannah, Mary is implicated in the vow of the Nazirite (requiring the mothers of Samson and Samuel not to consume fruit of the vine). So, in addition to Mary's vow: "I do not know man" (Luke 1:34), signifying her Jephthah-like vow of perpetual virginity, another vow is presupposed here; namely, Mary is similar to Samson's and Samuel's mother in a special class of women who had access to the Temple after making vows.

But how should we understand this term: "full of grace"? After all, the translation made famous by the Douai-Rheims Catholic Bible has been called into question, where "favor" is said to be a more accurate translation.[85] To answer, I begin by quoting Luke 1:29 from the AD 1611 King James Version of the Bible: "And the Angel came in unto her, and said, Haile thou that art highly favoured, the Lord is with thee: Blessed art thou among women." We can consult the Roman Catholic version of Luke 1:29 (AD 1582 Douai-Rheims): "And the Angel being ent(e)red in, said unto her: 'Haile, full of grace, our Lord is with thee: Blessed art though among women.'" Is there any opposition between the two most famous English Bibles on this question?

In answer, we compare: "highly favored" (1611 KJV) and "full of grace" (1582 Douai-Rheims). First, everyone agrees that the basic Greek root "*char-*" means either favor or grace. However, we do notice how funny it might sound if Paul's typical opening lines of an epistle should read thus: "The favor and peace

---

[85] See Brown, *Mary in the New Testament*, 126-128.

to you from God the Father of our Lord Jesus Christ!" (2 Corinthians 1:2). Everyone is used to: "The grace and peace to you from God the Father!" To settle the matter of grace/favor I take the evangelical principle of interpreting Scripture by Scripture. So let us use the only other passage in all of the Bible (even the King James 1611 version) that has the word "full of grace"; namely, Sirach 18:17 (1611, KJV): "Lo(e), is not a word (*logos*) better than a gift (*doma*)? But both are with a gracious (*kecharitôménôi*) man." What does gracious/gratious [*sic*] mean here? Well, the earliest English dictionaries (AD 1604-1617) don't contain "grace" or "gracious" or "favor" for us to know how the King James reader would have exactly defined favor and grace. However, the next closest English dictionaries (using the King's English), have this to say: "Gracious, endued with grace..." (Dictionarium Anglo-Brittanicum 1708) and "Gratious, kind, favourable ..." (Dictionarium Anglo-Brittanicum 1730). Also "grace" itself is defined as "favour, good-will..." (1708/1730). More interestingly, for religious texts, the Dictionary meaning of grace is as follows: "the Mercy of God in finding out means for the Redemption of Mankind, etc." and "a Power or Disposition to yield Obedience to the Divine Law" (1708). We end with this last term: "Favour is opposed to rigour, especially in matters of justice" (1708/1730). To our knowledge these are the closest and only dictionaries to define our Biblical terms.

As best as an English speaker can (from a dictionary), Mary received something like this message (Luke 1:29; per definitions of favor in KJV): "Greetings, woman who has been prior favored in justice [unlike rigor for other people] to personally yield by power or by your disposition obedience to the divine law." This looks a lot like "original justice." However, since for the KJV 1611 (in light of the 1708/1730 dictionaries), grace is favor and the term gracious means endued with grace. So, we could translate Luke 1:29 thus: "Greetings, woman who has been prior endued with grace of justice [unlike the rigor held for other people] to personally yield by power or by your disposition obedience to the divine law." Whether we pick KJV or the Rheims version, grace and favor are virtual equivalents. Hence, both translations are correct King's English and both suggest correctly that Mary was in position of justice unto obedience in her will (unlike Adam and his progeny) to carry out the Divine Law in a way that Adam and Even did not. Therefore, this looks exactly like Luke above, who quoted LXX Genesis 15:1-2, to signify that Mary is finally a just person worthy of fulfilling the prophecy to bear like Abraham a child of promise. However, unlike Sarah, she is a woman who does everything according to divine expectations.

The Greek term that is very much cited is *kecharitomenê*. This is in context the possession of original justice or being "highly favored" or being "full of grace" sometime before she was twelve years old. We would perhaps be cautious or skeptical to say "yes" even if "original justice" was lost by Adam and Eve, and although we have no Biblical event to tell us when Mary received this justice (except only that she possesses it before the Annunciation), it could hypothetically be the case that after conception but before the Annunciation some hidden restoration of original justice happened to Mary. Now, I mentioned that the term "highly favored/full of grace" is mentioned only in Sirach and in Luke. The Evangelist does seem to be aware of the fact, too, that up to his time other text in history known to him do not use this word outside the Bible. That's pretty significant. So why burden us with such a word? Only if we can see hints of its meaning in a religious book like Sirach can we account for its use in Luke 1:29. This will help us understand the history of the term "full of grace" eventually meaning "immaculate." Let's start with Sirach 18:15-17 (KJV 1611 –adapted spelling):

> My son, blemish not thy good deeds, neither use uncomfortable
> words when thou givest anything. Shall not the dew assuage the
> heat? So is a word better than a gift. Lo, is not a word better than
> a gift? But both are with a gracious (*kecharitōménōi*) man.

First, I should mention that King James 1611 version of this passage had to translate from the Greek. The original Hebrew was only found in pieces in 1898 and again at the discovery of the Dead Sea Scrolls. Sadly, the Hebrew for Sirach 18:15-17 is, so far as I can tell, missing in the Hebrew that survives. So, King James and we ourselves must rely on the Greek, as did St. Luke the Evangelist. (1.) Notice: "do not mix blemish (*mômon*) with your good deeds." This is not clearly typological but there comes a contrast: good deed and good word. If there is a good deed it can be ruined by a bad word or blemish. It is an interesting aside that one of Mary's traditional Greek names in the patristic period is *amômos* or unblemished that is translated usually as "immaculate." We could just as well translate this as: "child, do not make maculate your good deeds." (2.) Next, we read: "neither use uncomfortable (*lupen logōn*) words." Here's where early Christians will pick up the wordplay between Sirach and Luke and Genesis. First, Adam listened to both the bad words and followed the bad deed of Eve in Genesis (3:17). His punishment is to eat in uncomfortable/toilsome existence (*en lupais*). Even, in the Protoevangelium (Genesis 3:15), or prediction of a child/seed of promise who will crush Satan's head, Eve –by her explanation or word to God and her bad deed– will conceive children in discomforts (*téksêi tekna en lupais*) (Genesis 3:16).[86] The lesson here for a woman is that when God asks for an account of his command, Eve should say the proper and truthful responses or words and should have done the just deed so as to avoid what is uncomfortable in conceiving. (3.) Next, Sirach assures his child that an immaculate/unblemished word is even better than a gift or work, but that both word and good deed/gifts happen with the "gracious man." Per KJV 1611 in English, we could say that gracious means the "man who has been prior endued with grace of justice [unlike the rigor held for other people] to personally yield by power or by disposition obedience to the divine law." (4.) Finally, Mary is the fulfillment of both word and deed: First, the word (*logos*) of the Lord comes to her and she responds immaculately to conceive an immaculate Christ. Secondly, she obeys the divine will by her power or disposition "Let it be done to me according to thy word" (Luke 1:38). (5.) However, Luke the Evangelist might not only play on "full of grace" due to Sirach (the only place where he could have learned the word for the Bible), but he is also probably playing on Genesis 3:16, which says that maculate (dirty) speaking and doing by Eve will "conceive children (*tekna*) in discomfort," whereas Sirach tells his "child (*teknon*)" to avoid words and deeds of "discomfort," and Luke sums up both sources for Mary's conception by saying that –unlike Eve– Mary is "full of grace" or obedient by word and deed to God's command and therefore God says through Gabriel: "you will conceive (*teksêi huion*)" (Luke 1:31). We might be disappointed that Gabriel doesn't clearly refer to the Protoevangelium and Sirach with the term *teknon*, but also remember that Luke is weaving in Genesis chapter 18 and Judges chapter 13 where "you will conceive *a son*" is messianic. So, perhaps, this strikes a balance among the sources. In the end, Mary was justified before the Annunciation, and then, after the announcement of her word and her good deed, she sings the Magnificat upon the announcement of a child being conceived in her womb. So, unlike Eve, she conceives in joy not in discomfort. All in all, the Scriptures bear witness to what the Fathers poetically develop out of Luke 1:29-

---

[86] Mary's exemption from this sorrow is a central preoccupation in the first decades of the second century, as witnessed by possibly Essene-Jewish composer of the *Odes of Solomon*. See Anonymous, *The Cup of Milk (Ode 19)*, in *The Odes Project: The Earliest Christian Hymnbook: The Odes of Solomon*, trans. James Charlesworth (Eugene OR: Cascade Books 2009), 55: "The virgin became a mother with great mercies: and she labored and bore the son without pain, because it did not occur without purpose."

42, namely, Mary has original justice and no curse or sin of Eve, unlike all other people who are not "gracious" due to the rigor of divine justice.

The only other writing to use the word "full of grace/highly favored" is the *Protevangelium of James*, probably written in the late-first century or the first half of the second century. Of course, this orthodox Christian is notable for underlining Mary's holiness and sinlessness from the moment when she was conceived miraculously until the birth of Jesus. However, the anonymous (likely) Palestinian (perhaps formerly Jewish) author does not give us anymore insights into the meaning of "full of grace (*kecharitômenê*)." Instead, we must wait for the late-second century author St. Clement of Alexandria (*Paedagogus*, III.11.83.3). We see only that Clement identifies a very beautiful women to the eye of a man to be "full of grace," but this must be, by now, a colloquial use when looking at the period of his writing. In one other place he does give us new information. According to Clement, it is the *Holy Spirit* who makes one "full of grace" or "having been favored" (*Stromata*, I.1.14.1). However, real progress on the use of the term "full of grace" has to wait till Origen of Alexandria who writes early and in the middle of the third century. We finally get to see, like our English dictionaries, a full definition of "*kecharitômenê*." Origen writes:

> So, as virtue is a grace, which produces someone possessing fullness of grace (*kecharitômenon*), when this [grace] has continued onward prosperously by way of free choice in us; in these circumstances what is from God becomes present, and this is what it is to give grace for grace from God (*Gospel of John*, fragments 11).

Finally, we have a key to understanding Luke the Evangelist fully. Mary had virtue prior to the Annunciation, which is a grace productive of making somebody "gracious" or "full of grace" or "highly favored." Earlier in the same passage, the virtue was identified as divine faith. Hence, Mary was justified by faith prior to the Annunciation, just as we would expect from the KJV 1611 translation of Luke 1:29. This all comes together in Origen's *Fragments* on Luke's Gospel (fragment 21a) where Origen, just as I showed above, contrasts Eve's discomfort (*lupais*) at conception and Eve's cursed children to the joy (*chara*) of Mary's process and accomplishment of conception. This becomes standard fare for interpretation in the fourth century starting with Gregory Nyssa (*On the Canticle of Canticles*) and beyond. It is possibly in light of these associations that the early apocrypha, like

96

the third-century *Gospel of Bartholomew* (2.2-3), know Mary's default title as: "highly favored," as if it were her proper name: "full of grace" (*kecharitômenê*), as equated to "immaculate" (*amolyntos*). In this development, the term "full of grace" is restated by the anonymous fifth-century Ps-Ephrem everywhere as: All-immaculate (*Panachrante*), all-pure (*Panagne*), and even all-graced (*Pancharitôtate*).

At this point, the Biblical evidence points to Mary being someone who enjoys the virtue of justice, like Abraham, who is established by faith in a covenant with the Triune God of Genesis chapter 18. As such, it is a legitimate question to ask: "When did Mary receive this divine gift of justice"? If there was a state of peace and friendship between God and her prior to the Annunciation, does the Bible supply us with any evidence of when this would have happened? After all, in the earliest traditions, to say nothing of both Jewish and Roman law in force in the first centuries in Palestine, the Annunciation occurred when Mary was twelve (though some have been tempted to prioritize manuscripts of the *Protevangelium of James* that say she was fourteen years old). The answer to this curiosity will be found shortly in chapter 4 below that investigates in detail Mary's Magnificat.

3.2 The Annunciation, Prophecy and Overshadowing in Luke 1:30-38

The next themes are already familiar to us, to some extent, due to the prophetic material quoted in common by both Matthew and Luke in order to detail the events of the virgin birth as the fulfillment of the promise of Yahweh to save his people in Judges chapter 13 and in Isaiah chapter 7, where both cases involved an Israel under the domination of pagans to be released unto David's seed for its salvation. Below we see how the wonderchild is connected to prophecy fulfillment as developed by Luke's adaptation of his Scriptural paradigms:

MT Judges 13: 6, 24: The first prophecy of the seed of Abraham being son of God (*ben Elohim*) and from Nazareth/Nazirite	Luke 1:31: The prophecy of Judges 13:6, 24 as quoted by Isaiah 7:14 is repeated to Mary, who is a virgin. The boy's name means "he who saves" because Israel will be saved (from sin)

(LXX=) 2 Samuel 7:9: I shall make for you a great name. v. 13: I shall establish the throne of his kingdom forever. v.14: I shall be his father, and he will be my son. v. 16: And your house and your kingdom will be made sure forever[87]

Luke 1: 32a: He will be great and will be called Son of the Most High. 32b: And the Lord God will give him the throne of his father David. 33a: and he will be king over the House of Jacob forever. 33b: and there will be no end to his kingdom.

Judges 11:39: a woman **knew not man** and died in perpetual virginity due to a vow of Jephthah inspired by the Spirit of God

Luke 1:34: Mary said: "**I know not man**," as proven in chapter 1, to mean that she is the New Daughter of Jephthah: a virgin till death

LXX Judges 11:29-31: The Spirit of the Lord was born upon Jephthah who had made a vow to the Lord of his daughter's virginity as a holocaust

Luke 1:35: And the angel answered her: "The Holy Spirit will come upon you" the power of the Most High will overshadow you and the one born shall be called holy

LXX Judges 13:2-3, 9-13: There is a double annunciation (doublet) to the sterile woman to conceive and a second appearance of the same Angel of the Lord next to Manoah with the same message

Luke 1:(19-25,) 36: Elizabeth and Zechariah represent one of the two doublet prophecies "you shall bear a son," while Mary is the second person to receive a doublet prophecy modelled on Judges. Zechariah's annunciation, like Sarah's (Genesis chapter 18), is somewhat unsuccessful

MT/LXX Genesis 18:14: "Is anything too wonderful for the Lord? /Nothing is impossible for God"

Luke 1:37: "No discourse shall be impossible [that is, too wonderful,] for God." The prophecy of the wonderchild of Genesis 18:14 is fulfilled in Jesus. As Sarah hears about "too wonderful" at the annunciation of Isaac, Mary hears

---

[87] Brown, *The Birth of the Messiah*, 311.

about "too wonderful" by mention of the annunciation of Elizabeth.

1 Samuel 1:18: Hannah has a miraculous pregnancy after assuring her husband she is a Nazirite and slave of her household Lord. LXX Judges 11:37: The ever-virgin tells her Father Jephthah to sacrifice her according to his vow by the Spirit	Luke 1:38: Mary is the slave of God like Hannah and Like Jephthah's daughter says to Gabriel: "May it happen to me according to your word"

Clearly, Luke sees the prior pregnancies of angelic annunciation in the history of salvation as preparations for Mary's wonderchild. However, since we have seen the prophetic material in prior chapters, what is the significance of Mary's "overshadowing"? To answer, let us take a look at the most important artifact in the world to be overshadowed in the Temple, prior to Mary replacing –for Luke– the Ark of the Covenant; since her Son is the New Law, the New Manna, the New Sprout from Rod of Aaron, and the New Temple. The language of overshadowing was concentrated on the Temple:

LXX Exodus 40: 1-39 (*partim*):	**Luke 1: 35:**
The Lord spoke to Moses [...] "Set up the tent (*tên skênên*) of the Law and put there the Ark (*tên kibôton*) [...] and cover (*skepaseis*) the Ark with the curtain." [...] And Moses did all, just as the Lord commanded him [...] and a cloud (*hê nephalê*) covered the tent of the Law and the tent [she] was made filled of the Lord's glory. Moses was also not able to enter into the tent of the Law, because the cloud **was overshadowing** upon [her] the tent (*epeskiazen ep'autên*) [...] made full of the Lord's glory. Yet, whenever the cloud would rise from the tent, the sons of Israel moved off with their possessions [...] for the cloud was upon the tent during the day and far was upon it during the night	The angel [to Mary] answered her ' "The Holy Spirit will come upon you, and the power of the Most High **will overshadow** (*episkiasei*) you and the one born shall be called holy."

Mary provided the physical flesh or metaphorical skin-of-the-tent to Jesus. This is always to be associated with the glory of the Lord and to be accompanied by his presence. Contemporary scholarship affirms Luke chapter 1 as a clear arrangement of the infancy narrative in direct relation to the Temple and its worship.[88] While Moses and Joshua (LXX Deuteronomy 34:9), Elijah and Elisha (LXX Sirach 48:12) were technically "filled with the Spirit" in the Septuagint and Masoretic texts, the tent and Ark were uniquely filled with the divine cloud and glory itself, God's proper attribute. Later, Mary will, like the prophets and apostles, be "filled with the Spirit" at Pentecost (Acts 2:4) but only when she no longer is constantly at the side of Jesus, her glory, that same divine "glory" who once filled her, not at all like an inferior prophetic operation or influence. Luke designates Mary (Luke 1:35) to experience the "power" (*dynamis*) of God filling her womb. The Evangelist likely recalls Paul's epithets for Jesus, "Christ the power of God and the wisdom of God" (1 Cor 1:24).

"The glory of the Lord" unquestionably signifies a theophany (God showing himself to humans), whereby God reveals himself to a human onlooker. Exodus chapter 40 (above) cannot be read in isolation. Mosaic ritual worship of the Angel of the Lord (considered God-Lord in the guise of a man or angel) happened when Yahweh appeared as the Angel in the pillar of fire and cloud (LXX Exodus 13:21-22; 14:24), who led the Israelites out of Egypt. Exodus chapter 40 culminates in the theophany (God's self-revealing) from Exodus 16:19, whereby the people "come near before Yahweh" by looking upon the glory of Yahweh in the cloud. Of course, this will be reenacted by the overshadowing cloud that first was in Mary at the Transfiguration in Luke's Gospel! "The Law," mentioned multiply in Exodus chapter 40, was dictated to Moses on Sinai, where God was present in cloud and fire (Exodus 24:9-18). Scholars have firmly established that the first Israelite experiences of Yahweh culminate in the Lord's worship rituals dictated to Moses for the precincts of the tent and Ark.[89] Carrying out the Lord's ritual prescriptions typically results in the coming of the glory of the Lord, who is

---

[88] Brown, *The Jerome Biblical Commentary*, 123.

[89] Charles Gieschen, *Angelomorphic Christology: Antecedents & Early Evidence*, Arbeiten zur Geschichte…42 (Leiden: Brill, 1998), 78-80.

present in cloud and fire at the exercise of the priesthood. In subsequent times God's proper attribute of glory underwent greater anthropomorphisization (describing God in physical-human terms) in LXX Ezekiel 1:26-28. The glory of the Lord took the form of a man riding the divine chariot-throne of the cherubim. Furthermore, this man-like being is surrounded by fire and smoke. Finally, the glory of Yahweh *is* identified as the very man on the throne (LXX Ezekiel 1:28). It is all but impossible to avoid the conclusion that the Angel of the Lord and the glory-man of Ezekiel's vision are the same (cf. LXX Ezekiel 8:2). Afterwards, in the vision of Daniel, Christians of yore found their point of intersection between Jesus and "the glory of the Lord." If Jesus shares in or identifies with glory, then he must be the Angel of the Lord. In Daniel's vision, "a son of man" is seen coming on the clouds of heaven. The son of man is presented to "the ancient of days" and is given dominion, glory, and kingdom for eternity (compare: Revelation 4:11; 5:12-13; 7:12). Luke will also connect these Biblical passages of Mary's identity as the Ark of glory to the Transfiguration (!) (see Matthew chapter 17; Mark chapter 9; Luke chapter 9), as if a Marian feast.

Some early Christian communities (Jude 1:14) thought the apocryphal *Book of Enoch*[90] to be inspired, as it identified the son of man as Enoch, who had ascended into heaven. Within this same text, the ancient of days and "the son of man" interact (1 Enoch 48; 71) in a way that continues Ezekiel's and Daniel's imagery and even fuses it with the image of personal or humanized divine Wisdom (1 Enoch 48:6; 49:1).

In this vein, Dr. Gieschen writes: "One of the most intriguing angelomorphic [Angel-as-Yahweh's-Jesus] aspects of Wisdom in Wisdom of Solomon is its relationship to the divine throne."[91] The author establishes the following: (1.) Wisdom is hypostasized (personal) (LXX Proverbs 1:20; 8:1-36; 9:3-6), (2.) Through Wisdom the world was created (LXX Proverbs 8:22-31; 3:19-20), and (3.) Wisdom is distinct from God and creation (LXX Proverbs 8:22-31; cf. Sirach 1:9). Unsurprisingly, intertestamental literature placed Wisdom with the

---

[90] James Charlesworth, ed., *1 (Ethiopic Apocalypse of) Enoch*, in *The Old Testament Pseudepigrapha: Apocalyptic Literature and Testaments* (Garden City NY: Doubleday, 1983), 1:5-89.

[91] Gieschen, *Angelomorphic Christology*, 93.

angels and angelic descent because the working of any angel (Hebrew: *m.l.k*) means "sent":

> Wisdom could not find a place in which she could dwell; but a place was found for her in the heavens. Then wisdom went out to dwell with the children of men, but she found no dwelling place. So wisdom returned to her place and she settled permanently among the angels. (1 Enoch 42:1-2)

In his detailed exegesis of wisdom literature, Dr. Gieschen notes the angelic motif of Sirach 24:2. Wisdom is in the assembly of the Most High and elsewhere it is located "beside him" (LXX Proverbs 8:30; Sirach 1:8-9) as an angel. Wisdom is definitively equated to an Angel of Lord, being identified as the pillar of cloud and fire that led the Hebrews out of Egypt (LXX Wisdom 10:17). Eventually, Wisdom is revealed to possess fully divine character.[92] Luke's Jesus identified a sent-Wisdom (namely Jesus himself) with the prophetic sacrifice of Abel.[93] Luke likely has in the background the first-century intertestamental literature that attested to Wisdom as the first Angel (of the Lord) of creation responsible for forming the

---

[92] Ibid., 90-2. Compare Wisdom 7:21-29:

> Wisdom, the fashioner of things, taught me. For in her there is a spirit that is intelligent, holy, unique, manifold [...] distinct [...] penetrating through all the spirits that are intelligent and pure and most subtle [....] a breath and the power of God, and a pure emanation of the glory of the Almighty [...] a reflection of eternal light.

[93] Abel's sacrifice was consumed by theophanic fire; in vogue as late as Didymus the Blind. See Sebastian Brock, "Fire from Heaven," *Studia Patristica* 25 (1993), pp. 231-232. Cf.:

> The wisdom of God said: "I will send (*apostelô*) into the very prophets and apostles [...] and they will kill [...] some of them [...] that the spilt blood be demanded [compare Revelation 18:24] [...] from the foundation of the world [...] from Abel to Zachariah, slain between altar and house" (*tou thysiastêriou kai tou oikou*) (Luke 11:49-51).

second angel of Adam.[94] Therefore, the Annunciation (Luke 1:35) has a traditional formula: *Sent-Wisdom or Sent-Angel-of-the-Lord goes into the tent and onto the Ark-Mercy Seat and results in Yahweh-presence-glory*. This is what happens to Mary!

There is one last point that needs to be understood to know what is behind Luke chapter 1: God's self-revelation in the Septuagint and in Luke is by the Greek word "name" (*onoma*), or God's "power" (*dynamis*). Dr. Gieschen writes: "Name-theology developed in which God's presence with his people was described through expression involving dwelling of his *shem* [name], especially in the sanctuary [of the Temple with the tent and Ark in it].'[95] God established Mount Zion for his name to be invoked. God's presence filled the Holy of Holies (LXX 2 Chronicles 6:5; 1 Kings 5:5).

With respect to Mary, God's name was especially present on the Mercy Seat (*hilastêrion*) of the Ark (LXX Exodus 25:22), as when David received the Ark to prefigure Elizabeth's reception of Mary in the next verses (historically to hint at something better to come!) of Luke 1:35.[96] This will have implications below. For, if the inanimate Ark demands gifts and presents in honor of Yahweh, what more does the living Mother of God demand? "The name" of Yahweh is strangely just like a person, for it "comes" (Isaiah 30:27), it "is a strong tower" (LXX Proverbs 18:10), etc. "The name" (of Yahweh) was consistently understood in Jewish literature to be associated with the creative command: "Let there be [...]" (MT Genesis 1:3; 6, 14).[97] "The name" is that by means of which God created the world.[98] In fact, the name is explicitly understood to be the creator of heaven and

---

[94] See James Charlesworth, ed., *2 (Slavonic Apocalypse of) Enoch*, in *The Old Testament Pseudepigrapha: Apocalyptic Literature and Testaments* (Garden City NY: Doubleday, 1983), 102-221.

[95] Gieschen, *Angelomorphic Christology*, 72.

[96] (LXX=) 2 Samuel 6:2; 1 Chronicles 13:6.

[97] Gabriel and Mary's statements signify the eternity or creative effectiveness of God's "word" in Luke 1:37-38. This Jewish doctrine was upheld in Psalm 103; 148, emphasized in 1 Enoch 69.

[98] Gieschen, *Anthropomorphic Christology*, 74.

earth in the intertestamental literature (Jubilees 36:7; 1 Enoch 69:17-18). The divine name is also capable of being *in* a Sent-Angel: "My name is in him" (MT Exodus 23:20).

Naming Yahweh can bring about a theophany; it is typical for obtaining the name's power in the Psalms: "My help is in the name of the Lord, who made heaven and earth" (LXX Psalm 123:8). The authors of the New Testament knew the name's power, as for example: "At *the name* of Jesus every knee should bend in heaven on earth and under the earth" (Philippians 2:10).[99] Consequently, the overshadowing of Mary (the Ark) through the archangel Gabriel is understood by the fact that the Lord's name is "in him [Jesus]."[100] Later, in the New Testament, we will see the name saves in traditional language, as for example: "I will call on name of the Lord and I will be saved" (LXX Psalm 17:3)?

The name Gabriel translates into "power of God," appropriately qualifying him to explain to Mary what is "the power of the Most High" (Luke 1:35). Gabriel is also associated with creation in Jewish literature.[101] What is more, popular Christian literature of the second century (e.g. *The Ascension of Isaiah*) carried on tradition that Gabriel functioned as "the Angel of the Holy Spirit."[102] Lastly, Gabriel is significant, within intertestamental Jewish literature, for "overseeing the cherubim" (1 Enoch 20:7). It is possible that 1 Enoch exercised influence on the Evangelist Luke (1 Enoch 48:4; cf. Luke 2:32). Also, Rev. Dr. Brown notes that Luke appears to be aware of the Gospel of John's Logos/Word-theology and its theophanic accounts of Christ "the Word," whose flesh is the Temple (John 1:14;

---

[99] See also: "But these are written that you may believe that Jesus is the Messiah, the Son of God, and that by believing you may have life in his name" (John 20:31); "Always giving thanks to God the Father for everything, in the name of our Lord Jesus Christ" (Ephesians 5:20).

[100] This is word play in the Hebrew. When God sends his angel and puts his "name in him" (Exodus 23:20). Known angels (Michael, Gabriel, and Raphael) not only announce the presence of God but the last syllable in each of their names (*el*) means "God."

[101] Gieschen, *Angelomorphic Christology*, 133-134.

[102] Gieschen, *Angelomorphic Christology*, 231.

2:19).[103] John's Word-theology supposes that Jesus is the Word, who made an angel-like descent, was clothed, as the Ark had been clothed in skin-flesh of a tent, and claimed that –if his body be destroyed (like the first Temple[?])– he will be resurrected like the second Temple(?). Conspicuously, as the Ark of the *first* Temple disappeared or "arose to its place" (LXX 2 Chronicles 6:41; Psalm 131:8); so too will the enfleshed Word (of God) clothed in the tent (skin) and its Ark (Mary [!]).

Origen significantly affirmed a common early exegesis of Luke 1:35, wherein "the Power of the Most High" signifies Jesus the Son,[104] who performs a self-incarnation and is the agent sending his "overshadowing" Spirit.[105] Origen of Alexandria identified (c. 222) Christ with Old Testament Wisdom sent into the world, just as we saw with Jews and their literature.[106] Origen additionally asserted (c. 233) that Son-Power and Spirit were reducible to distinct powers of God.[107] Lastly, Origen was extremely attentive to Greek LXX vocabulary. After thoroughly investigating Origen's *Homilies on Luke* and his *On First Principles* and commentary on *Song of Songs*, Dr. Hirschaur convincingly concludes:

> Quoting and interpreting Lk 1:35, it seems that Origen distinguishes the overshadowing of the Most High and the very shadow of Christ...We say that the "overshadowing of the Most High" is precisely the overshadowing of the *Power* of the Most High, that is, the overshadowing of the Son himself, the Word.[108]

Origen's interpretation supposes "overshadowing" to be the function proper to a divine person. Besides the overshadowing of the Ark in Exodus chapter 40, Origen

---

[103] Brown, *The Jerome Biblical Commentary*, 120.

[104] Origen supposes 1 Corinthians 1:24: "Christ the power of God."

[105] Emmanuel Hirschauer, "Origen's Interpretation of Lk 1:35: 'The Power of the Most High will Overshadow You," *Scrinium* 4 (2008), p. 34.

[106] Hirschauer, "Origen's Interpretation of Lk 1:35," 36.

[107] Ibid.," 35.

[108] Ibid.," 39-40.

points to other passages of overshadowing in the Greek Bible used by Luke (LXX).[109] First, let us quote our Masoretic text's Psalm 118 but refer to it below in the Greek:

> Blessed is he who comes in the name of the Lord. From the house of the Lord we have blessed you. The Lord God *has appeared* (*epephanen*) to us. Organize together the festal procession in **protective overshadowings [of cloud]** (*pukazousin*) up to the horns of the altar. You are my God, and I will confess you; you are my God, and I will exalt you. (LXX Psalm 117:26-29)

Notice the presence of "the name of the Lord" and "the house of the Lord" as in Luke chapter 1. Also notice that the notion of *appearance* is an Angel-of-the-Lord moment, also known as a theophany or epiphany. Origen commentary on this passage is as follows:

> [Psalm 117, verse 26:] "Blessed is he who comes, etc." The Evangelists also extracted this phrase to be a prophecy about Christ...who "comes in the name of the Lord"...He is not indifferent about angels who come as the Lord's servants...and each of the angels says..."The Lord sent (*apesteile*) me." Yet, he is who comes "in the name of the Lord" and has been blessed. [Verse 27:] "The Lord God too has appeared to us, etc"...His act of coming is not to change place, but to be manifest (*epiphanênai*). Now, he exists invisible, formerly unseen. By the fact that he is the icon of the unseen God, after he took the form of a slave [cf. Phil 2], the Word became flesh, was seen, so that –after having appeared thus– he might lead us back through this knowledge to behold unto his glory, i.e., 'the glory of the Only begotten from the Father, full of grace and truth.' [Verse 28:] 'Organize together the festal procession among overshadowing branches (*en tois pukazouzin*), etc'[...] These "**overshadowing**" (*pukazonta*) items carry leafy branches and fruit [...] He says that the Cherubim "**overshadow**" (*episkiazonta*) the mercy seat (*to hilastêrion*). This is the meaning of '*pukazousin*,' for '*pukazein*' means 'to cover'

---

[109] Origen, *Selecta in Psalmos (fragmenta e catenis)* (*Patrologia Graeca* vol. 12, col. 1585).

(*skepein*). The Cherubim covered (*eskepon*) with their wings the mercy seat. (Ps 117:26-29, *Fragments*)

Origen's exegesis is hardly superficial.[110] Though the Hebrew or Masoretic Text only implies the (theophanic) appearance of light and procession of palms in hand, the Greek or Septuagint reads into the original Hebrew a full-fledged theophany, as the normal meaning of *pukazô* in Greek is to cast a protective shadow or to cover. Origen is on solid ground when he associates this meaning with the Psalm, since theophanic elements include: "the name of the Lord," "overshadowing-covering," and manifestation. *This would explain why we see a transition in Luke's Gospel from Mary the Ark and the Mercy Seat of Yahweh to Jesus's passion and descent into Jerusalem where they shout and process like Psalm 117 unto the altar of Jesus's sacrifice under overshadowing branches singing*: "Blessed is he who comes in the name of the Lord." Even this moment reminds us of the overshadowing presence of the "power of the Most High" (Jesus) in Mary's womb in Luke chapter 1 and is now sung at the transformation of bread and wine (like Mary's womb) into the body and blood of Jesus at the Christian Eucharistic Liturgy or Mass during the Eucharistic prayer.

Above, Origen recognized the pedigree of the (two) Cherubim claiming that "overshadowing" (*episkiazonta*) angels constitute the identity of the two Cherubim of Exodus 40, who overshadow (*suskiazonta*) according to the Luke's source. The Greek Old Testament, as Origen knew, was also quoted in Hebrews

---

[110] If Origen's authorship questions remain, the passage reflects exactly Origen's *mens* and Alexandrian tradition. See Origen, *Fragments, Corpus Christianorum Clavis Patrum Graecorum,* ed. M. Geerard (Turnhout: Brepols, 1983), 1:153 (# 1427). NB, Athanasius, *Exposition on Psalm 117* (*Patrologia Graeca* 27, col. 476, 480): "It is necessary that the help to pray by calling on the name, who is the enfleshed Word of God [...], an aid sent along (*parapepomenên*) from heaven."

This is ominously eucharistic; Athanasius later repeats Origen's doctrine of verses 27-9: "He fills the divine tent (*skenê*) [...] of the altar (*thysiastêriou*)...while Cherubim **overshadowing** (*pukazonta*) [...] **overshadowing** the mercy seat [...] that is, to cover (*skepein*). The Cherubim were covering the mercy seat with their wings."

9:1-5, as parallel with Luke 1:35. The implications are obvious when comparing all these texts:

LXX Exodus 25:20-2:	Epistle to the Hebrews 9:1-5:
Two Cherubim will stretch out their wings from above, together overshadowing (*suskiazontes*) with their wings the mercy seat, and their faces toward one another [...] The Cherubim's faces will be in the direction of the mercy seat [...] Place the mercy seat from above onto the Ark and place into the Ark the tablets of the Law [...] I will be known by you from that place above the mercy seat in the middle of two Cherubim, who are upon the Ark [...] just as I myself ordered.	Now, the first tent (*skenê*) was prepared in which there was the lampstand, and the table, and the proposition of breads, called the holy things. Then, afterward, the second curtain, called the tent, i.e., the Holy of Holies, which holds the golden altar and the Ark of the Covenant (*tên kibôton tês diathêkês*), which has been covered from everywhere in gold, in which a gold vessel holds the manna and in which is the rod of Aaron, which sprouted forth, and the tablets [...] Yet, over the Ark (*autês*) were glory's Cherubim, who "overshadows" (*kataskiazonta*) the mercy seat.

Origen knew and affirmed Hebrews as essentially Pauline and scriptural. Hence, calling the two Cherubim of the Ark the divine Son and Spirit is scripturally justified by him. The Epistle to the Hebrews intensifies the phraseology of Exodus chapter 40. "Glory's Cherubim" almost means that "cherubic" is a characteristic of divinity. This description perfectly harmonizes with the participle (*kataskiazonta*) to describe the Cherubim as intensely overshadowing the Ark. "Overshadowing" (*kataskios, -on*) is just as sacrosanct in the Greek Old Testament (LXX) as the term similar term "overshadow together (*suskiazô*)." For example, the Prophet Zachariah witnessed a full theophany with an Angel of the Lord riding a fiery horse between *two* mountains that casted a shadow over him forming a trinity of beings:

> I (Zachariah) saw the night and, behold, a man rode upon a fiery horse and this man stood in the middle of two mountains (*oreôn*) overshadowing (*kataskiôn*) him and behind him multitudinous white horses [...] And the angel in me was speaking, he said: "I will show you [...]" The man, who stood, answered in the middle

of the mountains and said to me: "These are the horses whom the Lord sent out (*eksapestalken*) to patrol the earth." (Zachariah 1:8-10)

The Epistle to the Hebrews interprets the Cherubim of Exodus chapter 40 like the two divine mountains that overshadow "the man" (Jesus), just mentioned in Zachariah. This can easily be transferred to Luke 1:35, for Gabriel's heralds the divine presence at the Annunciation, just as Zachariah's angel of the Lord (Yahweh) had been "in" the Prophet.[111]

3.3 Visitation: The New Daughter of Jephthah becomes the New Ark in Luke 1:39-45, 56

The vocation of Mary as the New Daughter of Jephthah leads her no longer to run around the hill country bewailing a non-productive virginity till death, but quite the opposite. However, Luke makes sure to mix his sentences using phraseology and vocabulary from both the travels of the Jephthah's virgin daughter and the Ark of Covenant. The definitive characterization of Mary as the New Ark carrying the New Manna, Law, and Aaronic Rod occurs especially in the following verses:

LXX Judges 11:37-38: Jephthah's daughter, due to a vow, goes to her	Luke 1:39: Mary goes to her neighbors, her cousins, who receive

---

[111] A singular New Testament instance of *episkiazô* records non-divine Peter bearing his "overshadowing shadow" (Acts 5:12). Peter patrols the Temple vicinity. Knowing his route, invalids lie in his path hoping that Peter's "shadow" (*skia*) "overshadow" (*episkiasêi*) them with marvels. This perhaps fulfills Zachariah 1:8-10, where the divine man sent his horses, themselves under overshadowing of two mountains, to patrol the earth. *Acts* 5 reports Peter, as 'angel of death,' to Ananias and Sapphira (as horses in LXX Zachariah 1:11). Afterward, Peter brings fear on the assembly in a phrase common to angelophany. At any rate, Peter has no role as Mary (Ark), but he possesses a shadow casting a shadow within a Temple motif. For the Jewish belief in Apostles as angels (cf. Isaiah 6:6), see Gieschen, *Angelomorphic Christology*, 176-80.

cousins to bewail perpetual virginity denying her line a child	her like the Ark and perpetual-virgin daughter of Jephthah
LXX Judges 18:11, 15: The Danites (extended family of Samson) enter a house of a priest to take possession of their inheritance, while no king of Israel exists. "In the past [God] humbled Naphtali" (Isaiah 9:1) but the Danites prophetically anticipate God "will honor Galilee" in a like manner (compare Luke 1:79)	Luke 1:40: And entered the house of Zachariah and greeted Elizabeth. This oblique citation from Judges underlines cousins of Mary and yet she lives in their house. Jesus takes possession of the hill country fulfilling the prophecy of Isaiah Naphtali to be fulfilled by an even in Galilee.
(LXX=) 2 Samuel 6:5, 15-16: David and the house of Israel played music before the Lord at the return of the Ark to Israel at its reception. David receives it with shouting and with leaping	Luke 1:41: Elizabeth heard the greeting of Mary, so that the babe leapt in her womb and Elizabeth is filled with the Holy Spirit.[112]
LXX Genesis 14:19-20: "Abram is blessed (*eulogêmenos*) to God most high and blessed is he." This forms the	Luke 1:42: Then, as a prophetess, Elizabeth raises her voice (*anephônêsen*) loudly saying: "Blessed are (*eulogêmenê*) you among

---

[112] Brown, *Mary in the New Testament*, 133, claims the following with respect to the alleged parallelism here: "This parallelism approaches fantasy when David's dancing before the Ark is compared to the leaping in Elizabeth's womb as she greets Mary." This rebuff may be prejudicial but –in light of the arguments up to Brown's time– a lack of credulity is merited on the grounds that scholars reported no vocabulary or obvious thematic overlap on vague allusion. Brown is responding (as he indicates) to prior scholarship. If we merely add another parallel passage forming a composite for Luke 1:41, then things look very different. See (LXX=) 1 Samuel 16:13: "And [Samuel] anointed him in the midst of his brethren, and the Spirit leapt upon (*ephêlato epi*) David from that day on." Instead of the Spirit leaping, John leaps receiving the Spirit. This allusion is secured by the fact that John was often mistaken for being the "anointed one" or messiah (Luke 7:22; John 1:20-22). Clearly, Luke's styling of John as a leaping David before the Ark classes him as a possible anointed in the line of David.

antique form of blessing incorporated by in Deuteronomy.[113]

women and blessed (*eulogêmenos*) is the fruit (*karpos*) of your womb!"

LXX Deuteronomy 7:12-13: Only the one who hears and keeps the word or commandments of the Lord will be loved by him and be blessed in the fruit of (her) womb.

LXX Deuteronomy 28:4, 6: "Blessed (*eulogêmena*) are the children (*ekgonia*) of your womb [...] Blessed are you in your comings and blessed are you in your goings"[114]

LXX Ruth 3:10, 14:17: "You are blessed (*eulogêmenê*) to God, o daughter [...] blessed among every tent of Judah and every people"[115]

(LXX=) 2 Samuel 6:10: David said: "How will the Ark of the Lord enter unto me?"	Luke 1:43: Elizabeth said: "Whence is this happening to me that the mother of my Lord should come to me?"
(LXX=) 2 Samuel 6:11: And the Ark of the Lord **rested** *three months in the home (oikoi)*	Luke 1:56: So, Mary **remained** with her *for three months and returned unto her own home (oikon)*.

The Annunciation and Incarnation themselves are simply newer events where the glory of Yahweh descends onto the Mercy Seat in cloud and overshadowing. Now the Mercy Seat is Mary's flesh or her womb.

---

[113] This paradigm is also affirmed by Brown, *Mary in the New Testament*, 136.

[114] This paradigm is also affirmed by Brown, *Mary in the New Testament*, 136.

[115] Compare the more distant: LXX Judges 5:24; LXX Judith 13:18.

Luke 1:42 is the end term of a very rich tradition. Abram was first called doubly blessed by Melchizedek. Next, the Greek Old Testament forms the near-literal paradigm for Mary by announcing that whoever keeps all the just precepts of God and is perfect in the law, such a one shall the Lord love:

> If you hear (*akousête*) these just decrees and guard (*phylaksête*) them, then the Lord your God will keep his covenant of love with you, as he swore to your ancestors. He will love you and bless (*eulogêsei*) you and increase your numbers. He will bless the fruit (*karpon*) of your womb (*tês koilias sou*) (Deuteronomy 7:12-13)

Mary is the fulfillment of the Old Law: She "hears the word and guards/keeps" (Luke 11:28) the commands of the Lord and, therefore, Elizabeth calls her "blessed" (*eulogêmenê*) in line with Deuteronomy 7:13. Mary then prophecies about herself that all people will call her blessed (*makariousin*) in fulfillment of Jesus's words (Luke 1:28). The only time in the Septuagint that a number of women *shall* (in futurity) bless a pure woman occurs as follows:

> My dove, my undefiled is but one; she is the only one of her mother, she is the elect one of her that conceived her. The daughters saw her and shall bless (*makariousin*) her; yea, the queens and the concubines, and they shall praise her (LXX Song of Songs 6:9)

God can fulfill in her (alone) the covenant of the seed of promise. Her womb is blessed with the wonderchild. Later in Deuteronomy (28:4, 6,) this blessing is expanded into a list of blessings, but it is specifically the doublet blessing that repeats the doublet first said of Abram in Genesis chapter 14:19-20.

Finally, we see that such a blessing, formerly said of only Abram, is given to Ruth who is named in Matthew's genealogy but not in Luke's. In the context of Mary, as New Tent of Witness or New Temple, it could be taken to mean not only that Mary is again the fulfillment of annunciation paradigms, beginning with Abram with her perfect justice according to God's law to merit the fulfillment of his covenant through her; but she –like Ruth– is blessed among all the tents of Judah. The implication for the savvy reader would be that she is the Tent of Witness where the remnant of Israel is still to be found. Even the cautious Rev. Dr. Brown has conceded that scholarship admits Elizabeth "raised her voice" (*anaphônêsen*) (Luke 1:42), signifying nothing less than exclusively Jewish

112

liturgical activity in the Greek Old Testament. But Rev. Dr. Brown concedes too little. All such passages, such as 1 Chronicles 15:28 and 16:4-5, 42, are specifically liturgical singing before the Ark. The only other mention, 2 Chronicles 5:13, uses the verb to speak of liturgical worship in the house of God leading to cloud and overshadowing before the Holy of Holies. The net result is clear, Luke (who admittedly shows no sign of knowing Hebrew), used the Septuagint like most New Testament authors as a source and, in the case of Luke 1:42, can only be read as having Elizabeth liturgically celebrate Mary's arrival at her house as if she were repeating David's liturgical reception of an Ark that is actively overshadowed by Yahweh.

Now, Luke 1:43 would perfectly transition from Ruth as the blessed one among the tents of Judah, since it is David who receives the Ark when it returns to Israel. Still, David wasn't readied to receive it, much like the city of David (Bethlehem) was not ready to receive Joseph and Mary in Luke's nativity narrative, since nobody prepared a lodging for them. Instead, before David's formal reception of the Ark into his city, he prepares an impromptu lodging for it at the house of Obededom in the hill country. Of course, Mary does the same. She first rested in the hills with her cousins before she is received into the city of David. They find out quickly that nobody had prepared a place for them. We can also remember at this point Elizabeth's miraculous conception earlier (Luke 1:24), for Luke told that story with one eye on (LXX=) 2 Samuel 6:12-13:

> The Lord blessed all the entire house of Obededom and all of his substance […] "The Lord blessed the home of Obededom and all of its substance *because of* **the Ark** of God" (*heneken tês kibôtou tou Theou*). (LXX 2 Sam 6:11-12)

When turning to Luke 1:56 in light of 2 Samuel 6 (as Luke desires that we should do), we note that the Baptist's conception (= blessing) is as forerunner or *for the sake of the Ark of God*. Thus, Elizabeth is blessed with child *for the sake of* fulfilling the type of Obededom's family and Jephthah's neighbors who received the Ark and Jephthah's daughter in the hills: "Whence this happening to me that the Mother of my Lord [Yahweh] should come to me?" The parallelism between Old and New Testament is exact.

Intriguingly, "Mother of God" registers as a rare title within the earliest patristic commentaries, even though "**the Mother** of God" (*hê mêtêr tou Theou*)" should naturally be an inference from the Evangelist's typology: "**the Ark** of God" (*hê kibôtos tou Theou*). This inference toward "Mother of God" becomes a written norm in the patristic tradition in which the earliest Greek Father whom I have found to express this verbal parallelism between "Ark of God" and "Mother of God" is potentially Ephrem the Syrian (c. 306-373).[116]

Concluding remarks:

Only two major objections exist to Mary being the fulfillment of Ark typology in Luke. They are summarized and affirmed by default in the works of the reigning expert on Marian passages in Luke's Gospel, namely, Rev. Dr. Brown. Because his scholarly credentials on the infancy Gospels have made his conclusions an industry standard, it is not fair to dismiss Rev. Dr. Brown without listing fully his concerns or doubts regarding Luke being styled a typological writer and promoter of Mary as the New Ark. I should state that Rev. Dr. Brown asserts that he is open to such typology. However, his major concern is that verbal parallels between the Greek Old Testament and Luke should not be overblown. A criterion for not exaggerating this overlap is what we can call: "exclusivity."[117] *If and only*

---

[116] Ephrem the Syrian (*graecus*), *Prayer* 8, in Ὁσίου Ἐφραίμ τοῦ Σύρου ἔργα, Ed. K.G. Phrantzoles (Vol 6; Thessaloniki: To Perivoli tis Panagias, 1995), 6:351.

[117] I agree and apply an important principle advocated by Brown, *Mary in the New Testament*, 130:

> Some methodological consideration are in order here. If the Greek term [in Luke] in question is not uncommon, one cannot assume that Luke borrowed it from the LXX; if it is common in the LXX, one must prove that Luke had one passage in mind rather than others; and one cannot assume that Luke had a concordance enabling him to relate all the passages containing the same term. And finally, even if a certain *possibility* is established of a subtle reference to the OT, one must still ask whether an audience would ever have understood such subtleties without clear indications by Luke.

The last caveat is stated, I believe, weakly. If Luke is on the one hand elevating style of his predecessors and, like Greek historians of his context and past, looking for models, then – in addition to being literate beyond a mere bureaucrat or merchant recording data – we should expect Luke to be much less accessible to readers in a poorly literate Greek world *if* a phrase is unique to the Septuagint and Luke alone can we immediately work toward establishing literary dependence. Even in this case, Luke's access and his relation to such material must be plausible in order to secure a connection. For example, if we hypothetically find a scrap of papyrus in Nubia, Africa, and it predates a singular phrase known only to Luke up to the first century, prior to the discovery of the aforementioned (contrary to fact) papyrus, then we still must establish reasons for thinking this is not just a case of coincidence.

Given the complexities of Greek –very different from English grammar and syntax– a scholar in Greek literature often finds that even famous writers' phrases are very rare and unique. (Meritorious or neutral) plagiarism is fairly easy to demonstrate (versus coincidence), since it is often very unlikely for an experienced scholar (who studies many verbatim Greek overlaps of some several words, whether exactly, or nearly exactly,) to find mere coincidence as the culprit. Yet, often there is evidence, or suspicion, of a no longer existent or extant mediator or missing link between two quotations separated by centuries, when it is clear that a dependent author did not directly imitate the phrase as it had initially occurred. These technicalities, however, are simplified here in order, at least, for the reader to understand that Rev. Dr. Brown need not be classified a skeptic for his caution. His objections generally do not reject Luke's dependence on Judges and 1-2 Samuel, for Rev. Dr. Brown explicitly argued such in several studies on Mary in the New Testament. Rather, Brown specifically takes issue with Mary as Ark of the Covenant for technical reasons. To be transparent, we think, since his estimation of the topic has dominated discussions since 1978 until present, it important to address his objections:[118]

Objection 1: The Transfiguration on Tabor represents another instance of the term overshadowing but is not obviously connected with Mary and with the Temple or Tabernacle/Tent of Witness where the Ark is housed.

Unfortunately, despite Rev. Dr. Brown's erudition, this is simply overlooking the mountain (pardon the pun) of evidence to the contrary. Let us recall that the force of the objection lies in the word: "overshadowing cloud"

---

and an unimaginative world of bureaucrats among many of the literate. Any and all subtle references by that fact would likely go over the heads of non-literary hearers and readers.

[118] See also a largely unchanged evaluation of the evidence decades later in Brown, *The Birth of the Messiah*, 344-345.

(*nefelê episkiazousa*) in Mark 9:7. As such, scholars note that both the stories of the baptism of Jesus and Transfiguration include *the motif* of a cloud, of an implied or explicit shadow and light, and of an announcement or vision of the Spirit and identification of Jesus as the Son of God. Of course, the coming of the Spirit and designation of Jesus as "Son of the Most High" in Luke chapter 1 looks like a perfect thematic overlap. The same picturesque overlap occurs at the Transfiguration. Hence, the argument is as follows: Because Marcan and Matthaean written stories of baptism and Transfiguration are older than Luke's infancy narrative, the original application of overshadowing had been to these events that don't suppose the Ark. Rev. Dr. Brown refers to some of the Old Testament overshadowings as we have, which show mountains and overshadowed men but do not obviously point toward the Ark or to its Tent.

In answer, the patristic literature before the First Ecumenical Council of Nicaea (but also after) (AD 325) especially keyed into our point that there are two beings in Luke 1:35: "the Holy Spirit" and "the power (=Jesus) of the Most High." The more recent scholarly literature on angelomorphic or Angel-Christ studies confirms the enduring value of this interpretation. This means that like Jewish interpretations and pre-Nicene Christians, two special beings are present at the sacred place of Yahweh's most intense presence. Rev. Dr. Brown ignores the pattern: There are typically a Trinity of beings: Two overshadowing mountains over a third being, or three overshadowing sacred trees, or three angels under the shade of Mamre. By Brown ignoring the pattern also in Luke 1:35, it is detrimental to his case and only reinforces Mary's claim to be another case of such a pattern. There is the Father in the cloud, the Spirit as dove, and Jesus in the water at Jesus's baptism. Likewise, we see that at Luke's Annunciation to Mary the divine beings are three: Father, Spirit, Power, while at Jesus's Baptism, they are: Father, dove, Jesus. If Luke or other Evangelists had wanted us to understand "overshadowing" in an explicit way at either the baptism or Transfiguration, why did they not use the available and specific word as Mark uniquely did for the Transfiguration? Why, also, did none of the Evangelists include the important and pervasive term (within the LXX) when describing the baptism? But what should we make of the Transfiguration in Mark? This is the one case that might justify Rev. Dr. Brown's reticence: The Father speaks with a voice, a cloud separately overshadows, and Jesus is resplendent with light and whitened (Mark 9:1-7). But in each version (Mark, Matthew, Luke) the story immediately and explicitly relates the Tabor experience to the Ark by its underlining the building of a Tent by Peter saying: "let us make three tents/tabernacles: one for You, one for Moses, and one for Elijah"

116

(Mark 9:5). Moses's and Elijah's tents are meant to form the camp around this central Tent, just as in the wandering of Israel in the desert. Notice, Jesus is at the center on a mountain and is flanked by two sent-messengers (angels[!]) of Yahweh, one of whom is definitely on God's heavenly throne (or automobile/chariot) and the other is by popular tradition thought (even if wrongly) to be assumed into heaven like Enoch and Elijah. They act just like the two cherubim flanking the Ark. However, all Evangelists make sure not to misidentify the two prophets as personally "overshadowing" Jesus. The cloud only is allowed to overshadow; so also the cherubim on the Ark (interpreted by Jews like Philo as divine beings) are overshadowing personally with their wings (divinely), but these two men (Moses, Elijah,) are only inferior substitutes or standing in for divine overshadowing. Hence, all Evangelists emphasize that the only shadow cast was by the cloud overhead. This makes sure not to elevate Moses and Elijah to the divine status of Jesus, the uniquely overshadowed being. The suggestion by Peter to build a central Tent for the overshadowing is clearly reminiscent of the Tent of Witness for encountering the overshadowing on the Mercy Seat of the Ark. Rev. Dr. Brown simply failed to examine the common patristic readings on these relationships and see how the Greek and Hebrew liturgical background all justify Luke's development of this theme. Luke takes up the special term "overshadowing" in his original materials or in his reading of Mark's Gospel and correctly transfers it to Mary. But he also conspicuously omits Mark's original and singular use of "overshadow" for the Transfiguration cloud. Luke (perhaps) relocates the all but singular term in the New Testament to exclusively one other place in his Gospel, to Mary's womb. Luke moves the paradigm chronologically to the earliest event in Jesus's presence on earth, prior to his baptism and Transfiguration. Even if Lukes's literary form is adapted from Mark, Luke does so in a way that prioritizes Ark imagery from Mark. This point is missed by the ordinarily perspicacious Rev. Dr. Brown.

Objection 2: David's question about the reception of the Ark could equally be from 2 Samuel 24:21. Let us compare the evidence:

And David feared (*ephobêthê*) the Lord, […] saying: ^{How} (*pôs*) shall the Ark of the Lord (*hê kibôtos kyriou*) come (εἰσελεύσεται) **to me** (*pros eme*)? ([LXX=] 2 Samuel 6:14)

And Arauna said: ^{For what} (*ti*) _{did} <u>my lord the king</u> (*ho kyrios mou ho basileus*) _{come} (*êlthen*) **to his servant** (*pros ton doulon autou*)? ([LXX=] 2 Samuel 24:25)

And ^{whence} (*pothen*) is it to me that <u>the mother of my Lord</u> (*hê mêtêr tou kyriou mou*) _{should come} (*elthêi*) **to me** (*pros eme*)? (Luke 1:43)

Again, given the fact that Rev. Dr. Brown does not deny other parallels between the Ark and Mary (for example, Luke 1:56, above), it is surprising that Rev. Dr. Brown uses such a rigid hermeneutic of suspicion against pro-Ark claims; based principally on the allegedly ambiguous source for this passage. However, despite Rev. Dr. Brown's youthful misgivings, he became more appreciative of the collective weight of counterarguments in his most famous work on the infancy narratives of the Gospels:

> We have not finished the discussion of Mary as the Ark of the Covenant, for it will reappear in the next scene of the visitation (Luke 1:43), even as will the theme of the Daughter of Zion. If the evidence thus far adduced for either symbolism is not convincing, the proponents argue that the evidence is cumulative. Let me reserve judgment. But in showing myself dubious thus far, I do not wish to convey the impression that in my opinion Luke did not think of Mary against the background of the OT.[119]

Indeed, unlike the simpler narratives known to Rev. Dr. Brown in his youth, we can add onto typological exegesis so many important differences between the allegedly competing passages for paternity of Luke 1:43. Mary came to the mountain and apparently ministered to Elizabeth in her more gravid state. So, Mary is the servant, not the Lord of the house (2 Samuel 24:25); Elizabeth is an old woman and mistress of the house. A citation of David's inferior servant, as if it represents Elizabeth, would be strange and make no sense. Since the Old Testament is literarily for Luke hardly what Shakespeare is to English speakers, Luke would have been better served by writing in his higher style to compose his story in his own words rather than use a Greek verse of negligible literary value

---

[119] Brown, *The birth of the Messiah*, 328.

that only serves to confuse a scholar familiar with the Greek Old Testament. Next, we see a stereotype –already affirmed by Rev. Dr. Brown– where annunciations normally start with fear, just like David's reception of the Ark, after which follows a good message and peace. 2 Samuel 6:14 fits Brown's own observations about stereotyped annunciations. The parallels between the "Ark of the Lord" and "Mother of the Lord" are very hard to dismiss, especially given other exact parallels within these and even other of Luke's verses. Even if 2 Samuel 6:14 were compared with 2 Samuel 24:25 and Luke 1:43 purely on its own merits, without the considerable contextual support of other pro-Ark verses in Luke, there is no reason to prefer 2 Samuel 24:25. In fact, to do so would merit quite a bit of criticism but the opposite is clearly not true. It is hard to avoid the impression the Rev. Dr. Brown was refusing to give the typologists a fair hearing and remained attached to rather weak arguments from his youth.

Chapter Four:

The Magnificat, the Purification, and the Wedding of Cana

4.1 The Magnificat Luke 1:28-29, 46-52

We saw in chapter 2 that Luke was the first person in the history of the Greek language to quote the lonely term: "full of grace" or "highly favored one" from the Greek version of the book of Sirach. Only after Luke embraced this term uniquely attested by Ben Sira (in Sirach) do Christians begin using it in the late-first and early-second centuries. About from eighty to ninety percent of the New Testament citations from the Old Testament come from the Greek version of the Jewish Bible and Luke was no exception.

We have already discussed in some detail the dependence of Luke 1:28 on Sirach. Maybe it is worthwhile reproducing the meat of the discussion to continue our discussing by using that rarest of vocabulary words. The term "highly favored/full of grace" is mentioned only in Sirach and in Luke. That is pretty significant. In fact, we might wonder if the preference for the "word" coming to Mary in Luke 1:29 plays on this in Sirach as well. Let us also repeat our previous citation of Sirach 18:15-17 (KJV 1611, adapting spelling,) in order to advance our discussion:

> My son, blemish not thy good deeds, neither use uncomfortable
> words when thou givest anything. Shall not the dew assuage the
> heat? So is a word better than a gift. Lo, is not a word better than
> a gift? But both are with a gracious (*kecharitômenôi*) man.

Now that we've reviewed the important points made by Sirach, we see the importance of Sirach to contextualize other verses of Luke (1:28-29, 1:46-52). We have already seen that the Archangel Gabriel brings news of Mary's possession of a word (the **word** of the Lord) and **grace** (not to mention of the upcoming wonderchild Jesus). In fact the term grace (*gratia* or *charis*) in the first-century

Roman empire, especially in Roman law as followed and commented on by Luke in Paul's trials under Roman officials in Acts of the Apostles, means a legal gift from the divine emperor. This is an added nuance to Luke's very Greco-Roman understanding of the term. Gabriel announced the gift to Mary of being "full of grace" prior to her acceptance of the divine word and a divine gift. Luke sets up Mary's song of celebration of her own holiness or humility by first having God reveal it to her by an angel by saying that she was already holy in the past and is still holy at the moment of his greeting:

| LXX Sirach 18:17: So is a **word** (*logos*) better than a gift [...] and both are with a *grace-filled* (*kecharitômenôi*) man. | Luke 1:28-29: Hail, you who have been full of grace (*kecharitômenê*) [...] Mary was troubled[120] with the **word** (*tôi logôi*) |

Now, the question of Mary's hymn or Magnificat is a complicated one without very much scholarly agreement, as Rev. Dr. Brown states: "There is [...] considerable disagreement about the classification of the poem."[121] Just about every aspect of the hymn is disputed. So, as per usual, let us go to Luke's sources in the Septuagint and see if we can find matching vocabulary and themes for the hymn to solve such puzzles!

Among the few things certain is that Hannah's hymn after her annunciation and conception of the prophet Samuel forms a rough outline or the literary form or style of speech that Mary utters. However, most scholars stop there. We notice, however, that for much of the vocabulary of Hannah's hymn there is quite a divergence from Mary's hymn or Magnificat. Not only this, but Luke's hymn is abbreviated in comparison to Hannah's length and it thematically turns toward the theme of holy conceptions and creations versus the oppression of the afflicted by Hannah's enemies.[122] How can we account for this? Is Luke claiming Mary sang this new song herself, or is Luke using artistic genius to recreate the substance of Mary's song? In answer, we need to turn to the very popular Sirach who was already cited by the Angel Gabriel's verse using the term

---

[120] Compare LXX Ruth 3:8-9; LXX Judith 14:7.

[121] Brown, *Mary in the New Testament*, 137.

[122] See Brown, *The Birth of the Messiah*, 348: "The Magnificat does not specifically apply to the situation of Mary and Jesus."

"full of grace." Mary's hymn is mainly a combination of the hymn of Hannah and a liturgical blessing in Sirach. Mary's hymn is no longer praising miraculous pregnancy that takes away the shame of an old sterile and childless women, but Mary sings her own praises (which is a vice in Hannah's hymn[!]) after Mary is praised by Elizabeth. Let us take a look at the chiasmus and my references to Luke's sources for each line of Mary's hymn (naturally relying on the Septuagint):[123]

A₁ Luke 1:41: And it happened, when Elizabeth **heard** (*êkousen*) the greeting of Mary, that the babe leaped in her womb _{in joy} (*en agalliasei*); and *Elizabeth was filled* (*eplêsthê*) *with the Holy Spirit.*

> **[1] Luke 1:42:** Then she spoke out with a loud voice and said (*eipen*):

>> **[a₁]** Blessed (*eulogêmenê*) are you among women and blessed is the fruit of your womb! But why is this granted to me, that the mother of my Lord should come to me?

>>> **[b₁]** ^{For behold} as soon as the voice of your greeting sounded in my ears, the babe leaped in my womb for joy.

>> **[a₂]** Blessed (*makaria*) is she who believed, for there will be a fulfillment of those things which were told her from the Lord."

> **[2] Luke 1:46:** And Mary said (*eipen*):

>> **B₁** MY SOUL MAGNIFIES (*megalynei*) THE LORD (*kyrion*) (1 Samuel 26:20-25; 1 Samuel 2:1-2) and _{my spirit rejoiced}

---

[123] For the objection to a similar but not same theory, see Brown, *The Birth of the Messiah,* 348, where Brown objects to the Lucan canticles to be Luke's compositions due to "Semiticisms" in the canticle. However, my demonstration of Luke's replacement of themes in Hannah's canticle with mainly passages from Sirach (and other LXX passages) explains Hebrew modes of discourse simply preserved according to the oft-stilted translations of the Septuagint.

(*êgalliasen*; quote from above A₁)[124] in God my Savior, for he has regarded the humility of his maidservant (1 Samuel 1:11).

[b₂] For behold henceforth all generations will call me blessed (*makariousin*; Canticles of Canticles 6:9), for he who is mighty has done great things for me (Job 5:8-11; Psalm 135:4-5; Sirach 50:22), and holy is his name (Psalm 111:9; Sirach 50:20) and his mercy is on those (Sirach 50:22; Ps 103:17) who fear him from generation to generation. He has shown strength with his arm (*kratos* [=*keras*]) (Sirach 47:5); He has scattered the proud in the imagination of their hearts (Sirach 10:14). He has put down the mighty from their thrones and exalted the lowly/humble (1 Samuel 2:5-7). He has filled (*eneplêsen*) the hungry with good things and the rich he has sent away empty (1 Samuel 2:10; Genesis 31:41-42; Deuteronomy 15:12-13). He has helped his servant Israel, in remembrance of his mercy, as he spoke to our fathers, to Abraham and to his seed forever (Sirach 50:23).

[3] Luke 1:56: And Mary remained with her about three months and returned to her house.

A₂ Luke 1:57: *Now Elizabeth's fulfilled (eplêsthê) the time for her to be delivered,* and she brought forth (*egennêsen*) a son. When her neighbors and relatives **heard** (*êkousan*)

B₂ Luke 1:58: how THE LORD MAGNIFIED (*emegalynen*) mercy to her, they rejoiced with her.

Mary clearly shines as "full of grace": While Rev. Dr. Brown admits that "full of grace" is a possible translation of *kecharitômenê*, he believes little evidence leads us to prefer such a reading.[125] To the contrary, after looking at the chiasmus [A₁, A₂, b₂, above], Luke is in-your-face with the word "full." When God gives a gift

---

[124] Compare Habakkuk 3:18 as in Brown, *The Birth of the Messiah*, 358.

[125] Brown, *Mary in the New Testament*, 126-127.

to Mary and Elizabeth in Luke's Gospel, he notably gives it "fully." We cannot expect scholars to catch everything in a text, but it is surprising that Rev. Dr. Brown plays down "full of grace," when the two women's poems above are about either Elizabeth or Mary and overflowing with the supernatural as the result of, or after, the Annunciation!

Luke's chiasmus has other features: Elizabeth "hears" and her neighbors "hear" [A₁, A₂]. Next, [A₁ & A₂ above] both extremes of the chiasmus begin and end with the notion of "filling" with respect to a baby in utero (Luke 1:41, 57). "Filling" is repeated a third time in the middle of Mary's Magnificat (Luke 1:53). This is hardly random. This matches Hannah's hymn (just above) in an important way. Hannah anticipated Mary's hymn (quoted below), saying: "*My horn is exalted* [that is, I am protected and delivered from enemies and have peace]."[126] Hannah's miraculous conception in her sterility quiets her mockers. Hannah's poem, quoted in full below, ends by reference to "exalting the horn of your christ (messiah)." Now, "exalting a horn" does not mean "to become pregnant" but Hannah's words in her hymn's first and last verse uncontestably develop in this case from her pregnancy as a sign of God's victory but her closing lines can be read as an anticipation of some other humble-sterile (wordplay) female (Mary) whose horn will be raised up to bear the messiah. Luke interprets Hannah's verses exactly in this way. Under the influence of the Spirit, referring to Hannah's verses about the future christ (1 Samuel 2:10), Zachariah prophesies: "Blessed is the Lord God of Israel, for he has visited and redeemed his people and has raised up a horn of salvation for us in the house of his servant David" (Luke 1:68-69). According to Luke, Jesus's future conception had been prophesized by Hannah.

Much of the Scriptural inspiration for Mary's hymn has already been suggested by Rev. Dr. Brown. Although we differ from each other in some places, we coincide on many Scripture citations. Our new contribution is mostly adding to Luke's repertoire an uncanny amount of Greek vocabulary and themes found in Sirach. While some of this was noticed by previous scholars, we believe that the liturgical blessing of the congregation in Sirach 50:19-24 pairs nicely with the incontestable citation "full of grace" from Sirach 18:17. Sirach accounts for some of Luke's rearrangement of vocabulary and themes from Hannah's hymn into

---

[126] For the complete meaning of this phrase, see Andrew Schmutzer and Randall Gauthier, "The Identity of 'Horn' in Psalm 148:14a: An Exegetical Investigation in the MT and LXX Versions," *Bulletin for Biblical Research* 19.2 (2009): 161-183.

Mary's personal song that is on a very different topic, as already noted by scholars. There are some thematic items that recommend Sirach to Luke's attention. For example, there is a double mention of "they blessed again […] and now bless" in Sirach 50:21-22. Also, Sirach shares with Proverbs a sense of humility meaning "virtue." In addition to Elizabeth calling Mary blessed twice and referring to her as fortunate or blessed yet a third time and Sirach coinciding with a triple mention of benediction, Sirach 50:19 echoes the vocabulary of "the Most High" already seen at Mary's Annunciation. Next, Sirach speaks of the liturgical blessing being perfected (*eteleiôsan*) and Mary (Luke 1:46) believes Gabriel's blessing will come to perfection (*teleiôsis*). Mary's faith or trust (Luke 1:28) is reflected by a cognate in Ben Sira speaking of believing (*empisteusai*) God's mercy to be with Israel. Turning to a fuller comparison, we show the common phrases or vocabulary hared between and among these three texts (that is, **bolded** letters **a.-r.**):

Luke 1:46-55:	(LXX=) 1 Samuel 1:9; 2:1-8, 10:	Sirach 50:21-24:
[Verse:] [46]: [a.] And Mary said (*kai eipen*): [b.] My soul magnifies (megalynei) the Lord , [47] [c.] And rejoiced (*ègalliasen*) [d.] my spirit in God my savior [48] [e.] for he has looked on (epeblepsen) the humility (tapeinôsin) of his maidservant, [f.] for behold henceforth all generation will call me blessed (μακαριοῦσίν)· [49] [g.] for he who is mighty did great things for me (epoiêsen moi megala) [h.] and holy is his name (hagion to onoma autou), [50] [i.] and his mercy is on those who fear him [j.] [51]	[Chapter 1, verse:] [9] [e.] Look on (*epiblepsêis*) the sterility-humility (*tapeinôsin*) of your maidservant [Chapter 2, verse:] [1]: [a.] And Hannah prayed and said (*kai eipen*) [b.] My heart rejoices in the Lord, my horn is exalted (*hypsôthê*) in the Lord. I smile at my enemies because [c.] I rejoice [d.] in your salvation, [2] [h.] because no one is holy (*hagios*) like the Lord […] [3] [f.] Talk no more very proudly: let no arrogance come from your mouth, for the	[Verse:] [18] And the people in prayer besought the Lord the Most High, until the worship of the Lord was perfected, and they had finished (*eteleiôsan*) their office. [j] [21] Then coming down he lifted up his hands over the congregation of the children of Israel [a.] to give glory to God with his lips and [h.] and to glory in his name (*en onomati autou*) […] and they blessed again […] [22] and now bless (*eulogêsate*) [g.] the God of all, who hath done great things (*ton megala*

125

he has shown strength with his arm, [k.] he has scattered the proud (hyperêphanous) in the imagination of their hearts ·[l.] [52] He has put down the might from their thrones [m.] and exalted the lowly/humble (hypsôsen tapeinous), [53] [n.] He has filled (eneplêsen) the hungry with good things [o.] and the rich he has sent away empty (kenous). [54] [p.] he has helped his child Israel (paidos), [q.] in remembrance of his mercy, [r.] [55] as he spoke to our fathers to Abraham and to his seed forever.

Lord is the God of knowledge and by him are actions weighted. [4] [l.] The bows of the mighty men are broken and those who stumbled are girded with strength. […] [5] [n.] Those who were full (plêreis) have hired themselves out for bread and the hungry (oi peinôntes) have ceased to hunger. [m.] Even the barren has born seven and she who has many children has become feeble. [6] The kills and makes alive [7] The Lord makes poor and makes rich, [m] he brings low and lifts up (tapeinoi kai anypsoi). [8] He raises the poor from the earth and lifts the beggar from the dung heap […] [10] […] He will give strength to his king(s) and raise the horn of his anointed (hypsôsei keras christou autou).

poiounta) in all the earth [m.] who raises our days from our mothers' womb (ton hypsounta hêmeras êmôn ek mêtras) and [i.] who does with us according to his mercy. [d.] [23] May he gift (dôêi) us [c.] joyfulness (euphrosynên) [d.] of heart [p.] and [gift] that there come about peace in our days in Israel [r] by the measure of the days of eternity (tou aiônos)· [24] to believe (empisteusai) [q.] his mercy [to be] with us [d.] to deliver (lytrôsasthô) us in our days.

Luke 1:46-47: If Mary's hymn were from a sterile woman who felt bereft of honor, then she would do well to repeat Hannah's phrase. Yet, Luke clearly does not equate the shame of an aged woman's sterility with the lot of being a youthful virgin. It is curious that Rev. Dr. Brown gratuitously asserts this in his magisterial study on the Magnificat. Luke, showing no signs of familiarity with a Semitic language, would not have encountered such an association in Greco-Roman society where there are numerous cases of honorable virginity (most famously the Vestal Virgins). The Septuagint never associates the Hebrew concept of sterility/humility (*tapeinôsis*) with a virgin, as if she were somehow a barren embarrassment.[127] Rev. Dr. Brown argues that Mary's hymn has a dual thrust: (1.) Mary is "barren" [*sic*(!)] and wants a child,[128] and (2.) The hymn pushes a sort of ancient liberation theology of the poor.[129] Of course, the first is completely without foundation in the Old Testament or Luke's culture, while the second –though intriguing– risks projecting an attractive fad of Roman Catholic theology from the twentieth century (*teología de la liberacion*) onto Mary. We seek to improve on Brown's reading by recourse to Luke's sources.

First, it should be noted that LXX Daniel 3:87 forms one principle link between sterility/humility (*tapeinôsis*), where youthful virgins sing a hymn as virtuously humble. Daniel renders these youths who have not defiled themselves with women and unclean food: "holy and humble in heart." This sounds very close to the meaning of Mary's sense in the Magnificat. Again, she is either twelve or fourteen years old.[130] It is amazing that Rev. Dr. Brown (who denies any vow by Mary of perpetual virginity in Luke 1:34)[131] thinks Mary is singing about her deliverance from the affliction of sterility at twelve-years old! *If* Rev. Dr. Brown had been fortunate enough to happen upon Judges 11:39 –proving Mary's perpetual vow of virginity– he could have formed a more convincing hypothesis: Mary sings her hymn (purportedly) because she no longer mourns her perpetual

---

[127] Brown, *Mary in the New Testament*, 139, also admits that scholars have evidence to argue (unsuccessfully) that the Magnificat is a hymn by Elizabeth, since it is Elizabeth (not Mary) who fit the themes of lowliness-sterility. Hence, there is an admission by scholars that Mary cannot be thought to complain about her lack of children.

[128] Brown, *The Birth of the Messiah*, 361.

[129] Ibid., *Mary in the New Testament*, 141-142.

[130] *Protevangelium*, 8.12.

[131] Brown, *The Birth of the Messiah*, 305-306: "There is no indication whatsoever that any New Testament author had an interest in Mary's marital relations after Jesus was born. Such interest is the hallmark of a later Christianity and cannot plausibly be invoked to interpret a crucial verse [1:34] in the annunciation scene."

virginity as Jephthah's curse, since she will have a child and keep her virginity to boot! However, Rev. Dr. Brown already closed this avenue. It is also noteworthy that the books of the Greek Old Testament translated nearest to the time of Luke increasingly identify humility (which word in Hebrew can infer sterility) as the opposite of hubris (*hubris*) or pride (Proverbs 3:34; 16:2; 29:23). By wisdom of a humble person God will raise up (*anypsôsei*) such a one's head to sit above powerful persons (Sirach 11:1). Likewise, Mary's own meaning should be obvious from her hymn: "He has scattered the proud in the imagination of their hearts (compare Sirach 10:14)." Mary is not a liberation theologian –as relevant as that might be to modern day oppression of the poor– pitting the poor against the rich in her hymn. What is more, we saw between Matthew and Luke many more lines and sources in common than is ordinarily noticed in the nativity narratives and Mary might have possibly been classed among the rich in their common sources, after receiving gold, frankincense and myrrh! Instead, Mary is celebrating her humility, inspired by Elizabeth, and Mary references themes closest to her own time when using the term "humility" within Proverbs and Sirach: God humiliated kings of the past by means of humble servants who lacked political and military resources of proud kings. Mary, in the lineage of David, does likewise by her virtue in welcoming her vocation as the mother of the messiah.

So, Mary's version of Hannah's song *must* avoid overtones of sterility for which Hannah was badly maligned by others in her old age. Mary equivocates Hannah's term, using Hannah's multifaceted word "humble," to signify a person about to be raised from her humility of spirit to on high to sit with her head above the greats (Sirach 10:14), and Mary substitutes for Hannah's words a unique quote from her ancestor David who was first in Mary's kingly line to put down a proud king Saul who was hunting to kill David (not unlike Herod who shall hunt to kill the Davidid family of Jesus in Matthew's Gospel):

> [David:] "The king of Israel has come out to look for a flea—as one hunts a partridge in the mountains." Then Saul said, "I have sinned. Come back, David my son. Because you [...][spared] my life today [not killing me when you had the chance], I will not try to harm you again. Surely I have acted like a fool and have been terribly wrong." [...] [David:] "The Lord rewards everyone for their justice (*dikaiosynês*) and faith (*pistin*). And behold as your soul was made great before my eyes in this today, though I would not lay a hand on the Lord's anointed/messiah, in just this way has

my soul gained great glory today, so may the Lord value my life and deliver me from all trouble." Then Saul said to David, "May you be blessed (*eulogêmenos su*), David my son; you will do great things and surely triumph."

"My soul magnifies (*megalynei*) the Lord" (1 Samuel 26:20-25; 1 Samuel 2:1-2) are the words of David replacing those of Hannah, as also detected by the first-century biography of Mary *The Protevangelium*.[132] Mary, like her ancestor David, shall dethrone her enemies by her offspring without violence. Secondly, Mary's justice (*dikaiosynês*) and faith (*pistin*) are exactly the theme of merit affirmed by Gabriel prior to revealing his prophecy. David, though originally using an idiomatic phrase in Hebrew, was translated into Greek in the passive voice to say: "My soul gained great glory." Mary actively glorifies or "exalts" God in virtue of her soul's operations in the present tense. This contrasts Mary's next statement that differs from Hannah's by Mary changing from the present to the past tense: "and my spirit rejoiced (*êgalliasen*) in God my Savior, for he regarded the humility of his maidservant." (1 Samuel 1:11). Rev. Dr. Brown and his group of scholars found this inexplicable. How can Mary talk about the deeds of God in her life in the remote past at twelve years old? Surely, they muse, this is a case of Luke using a prefabricated hymn and poorly adapting it to the situation? After all, Jesus will accomplish only all these things mentioned in the Magnificat for the poor, against kings, and for the lost by his Resurrection thirty-three years hence. Scholars then suppose that this is a retrojection or displacement of a hymn that really reflects something Mary would have better sung after the Resurrection, *not* after the Annunciation.[133]

Of course, this scholarly theory provides a very complex explanation to try to account for difficult features of the Magnificat working under the assumption that Mary's reference to her own past cannot be accurate. However, a simpler and textually based explanation could clear up Rev. Dr. Brown & Co.'s difficulties. Stylistically, just prior to Elizabeth's first line of Luke's chiasmus [A_1], begins a

---

[132] *Protevangelium*, 5.8.

[133] Brown, *Mary in the New Testament*, 139-140, notes that May can appropriately talk about what God has accomplished for her yet, since Jesus is not born. So, it is consequently argued that no reason exists for Mary to speak about what God has done for her in the past.

series of verbs, starting with a question in the present tense that Mary is supposed to answer: "[present:] From what place/stock [is] this that the mother of my Lord **should come** to me? [past #1:] For behold as soon as the voice of your greeting **sounded** in my ears, [past #2:] the babe **leaped** in my womb for joy. [past #3, future:] Blessed is she **who believed**, for there **will be a fulfillment** of those things which were told her from the Lord " (Luke 1:43-45). Notice, Elizabeth under the Spirit practically sidesteps the real presence of the divine christ, dedicated to God from his mother's womb, and asks Mary *about Mary*. She's the star to be honored despite the presence of the creator of heaven and earth! What a strange exaggeration of Mary's importance. Shouldn't this signify that the entire Magnificat is asking about *Mary's origins* her *bloodline* her *conception and birth*?

Mary's answer to Elizabeth follows in kind by present, past, and future sentences: "[present:] My soul **magnifies** the Lord and [past #1:] my spirit **rejoiced** in God my Savior. [past #2:] For he **regarded** the humility of his maidservant; For behold, [future:] henceforth, all generations **will call** me blessed" (Luke 1:46-48). If we compare Hannah's (LXX) hymn, we immediately infer that Hannah cannot be the pattern of the Magnificat's tenses: "My heart **was** [...] My horn **was**, [etc.]" (1 Samuel 2:1). Mary parallels Hannah's hymn only insofar as "heart" and "horn" are paralleled by Mary's "soul" and "spirit" (Luke 1:46) but the Old Testament tenses do not match Elizabeth and Mary (whether in Hebrew aspect or Greek time). So, in conclusion, Elizabeth's question (possibly meaning "whence" or "from what bloodline" or merely expresses surprise[!]) has an answer. Mary says that she presently comes from David's humble bloodline and from his house by quoting David's words to Saul meriting for David God's favor to be the new king and messiah of Israel. Mary then replies to Elizabeth telling her about her youthful past prior to Elizabeth's experiences, namely, Elizabeth's hearing Mary's voice her child John leapt in utero "in joy." As Rev. Dr. Brown has already noted, Mary's Magnificat for some reason quotes or retweets the "joy" of Elizabeth's in utero baby, when Mary turns to her own past tense, she is saying of herself that she had had the same experience as Elizabeth. That is, John the Baptist, while Elizabeth "was filled with the Holy Spirit," jumped for joy in utero. But when exactly did Mary's "spirit" ever jump "for joy" in utero? When was Mary saved from dangers in the past by God her savior? We don't know exact details from Luke's Gospel, but it's clear that Mary is taking her point of departure from Elizabeth in her comments about such a phenomenon: "I, Mary, also had the in

130

utero grace-filled experience!"[134] Rev. Dr. Brown unconsciously confirms our reading when he says of the past tenses used by Mary: "Once again the past tense (a bit awkward from the viewpoint that Jesus has not yet been born) represents the viewpoint of post-resurrection believers."[135] A Greek reader (who does not see a post-Resurrection projection in the text) would naturally be led by curiosity to know more about Mary's conception. This potentially leads to the composition of Mary's first biography in the late-first or early-second century called the *Protevangelium of James*. The Greek Christian reading the Magnificat saw this very thing: Mary is singing about her conception and birth. Finally, Mary completes her discourse by moving from the completed past to the future tense in line with Elizabeth's future blessing of Mary some lines prior. Elizabeth states that because Mary believed at the Annunciation that there shall be a child of promise and she shall be made by God fortunate (compare Luke 1:45; Genesis 18:14).

We should mention that Mary's reference to a savior is much discussed. God must be her protective savior but –like the Bible– he is a safety from past, present, and future danger just as for David, Mary's seminal predecessor. Notice, however, Luke's editing process, when choosing between Hannah's reference to God as a *savior* from external dangers and Sirach, who refers to sons of Israel needing a *redeemer* (from sin). The "great things" done by God are preventive and anticipatory deliverances from danger. By saying that "He has done great things *for my sake*" Mary is speaking not directly of the child Jesus in utero (as Rev. Dr. Brown & Co. agree) but of some peculiar grace or wonder given to her like the Baptist in utero. The most obvious sense would be that God created her as a marvel or miracle (this would justify her miraculous mode of conception by the *Protevangelium of James*). However, if it is argued that the "for me" is ethical, it means that Mary had miracles and marvels made for *her sake*, that is, that there is some sort of primacy of Mary as an object or goal of God's interventions and miracles into the world to honor Mary. Both choices lead to an understandable development in later Christian theology of the early life of Mary and the Fathers of the Greek, Latin, and Syriac traditions. In Mary's case, God would apparently be saving her from danger and creating her pure in some application of mercy or

---

[134] Brown, *The Birth of the Messiah*, 364.

[135] Ibid., 364-365.

compassion.[136] God's mercy (for sin) is specifically for those *who fear him*, but (in agreement with Rev. Dr. Brown) Mary's command by Archangel Gabriel is "Don't fear (*mê phobou*)." A savior in the Old Testament is uncontestably needed for extrinsic dangers and its meaning does not refer to a moral saving from sin. Sin is usually a case that leads Israel as a nation to national-political captivity and, needing "redemption" from their sins against Yahweh.

Luke 1:48-51: What does Mary mean, saying: "He has regarded the humility of his handmaid"? Despite the many merits of Rev. Dr. Brown and his laudably ecumenical team of Biblicists, we are left disappointed: Rev. Dr. Brown wants us to believe that the meaning of *tapeinê* (lowly-sterile-humble) in the original culture of the Hebrew Pentateuch (perhaps of the early-first millennium BC), as invoked by Hannah, should exactly account for the meaning for Mary. At first glance, we of course should be open to this, for Rev. Dr. Brown is referencing the Septuagint known to Luke. However, such Old Testament arcane references are typically to: (1.) lowliness-humility of economic status, (2.) blemishes-humility on women that merit them Mosaic legal sanctions, and (3.) sterility-humility of aged childless women. Depending on how disenfranchised we consider a professional laborer like Joseph, we might admit Mary membership in an oppressed class. Of course, skilled labor and Joseph's physical property or house, of which he is the head, in the Synoptic Gospels make this assertion tenuous at best. How exactly does Mary represent the hungry, oppressed poor, and their empty stomachs? After all, Joseph was head of and owned a house. Secondly, no scholar claims that Mary is a ritually impure woman by being *tapeinê* in the sense of the Mosaic Law. Thirdly, Rev. Dr. Brown becomes rather imaginative by claiming that Luke believes twelve-year old marriageable virgins have the same psychological complexes about childbearing as aged-married childless wives in Israel. He supplies no ancient or scholarly sources for his assertion.

In reality, Luke's Mary transforms –as admitted by scholars– Hannah's hymn: Sometimes Mary imitates Hannah's form of discourse, sometimes her vocabulary, and sometimes she quotes her verbatim. The citation of Hannah, where Mary speaks of herself as a humble handmaid, who has been looked upon by God, is no longer a reference to a Nazirite vow by Hannah to alleviate continuous

---

[136] See LXX Psalm 105:21 (deliverance from Egypt with "saving" from danger) and Ps. 135:3, 6 (making of heavens, and "the lights (sun/moon)" with "mercy"). Compare: Job 9:9 (rain/dew upon the earth); Daniel 4:37 (marvelous things on the earth).

132

sterility, but Mary uses the more recent Biblical and first-century notion of humility as a virtue opposed to "pride," which we have clearly shown, along with her perpetual vow of virginity. The problem lies in the fact that Mary is responding to Elizabeth's discourse: When is this humility looked upon by God? It is no longer in reference to Hannah's prolonged state of sterility but to Mary's youthful situation, as is obvious in Greek so puzzling to scholars. It is referring to her own remote past. How remote can this virtue be? We don't explicitly know from Luke. We merely know it already existed prior to the Gabriel's message. Mary seems to indicate that it was when her "spirit rejoiced" or –like John the Baptist– when she was in her own mother's womb. This will be better demonstrated as we see the same theme, time and again, come up throughout the lines of the Magnificat.

For now, we turn to: [b₂] "For behold henceforth all generations will call me blessed (*makariousin*; Song of Songs 6:9), for he who is mighty did great things for me (Job 5:8-11; Psalm 135:4-5; Sirach 50:22), and holy is his name." Elizabeth first finished her discourse prior to the Magnificat by referring to a future event of prophecy. Surprisingly, in reply to Elizabeth's prophecy about the future, Mary seems to join gratuitously her own fame to this event! That doesn't look like humility but more like pride to an inattentive reader! However, here, Mary is alerting her listener that she's very different from Hannah, who says: "Talk no more very proudly: let no arrogance come from your mouth, for the Lord is the God of knowledge and by him are actions weighted" (1 Samuel 2:3). So, how can Mary boast, when Hannah is exhorting humans that God judges the virtue of each of their works? Naturally, Mary's works are just due to the presence of the Spirit. But this is only a partial answer, for Mary boldly asserts that she shall be called fortunate or blessed according to the only instance of women calling a woman so fortunate in the future tense in the Old Testament:

> My dove (*peristera*), my undefiled/blameless (*teleia* [= Hebrew: *tām*]) is but one; she is the only one of her mother, she is the elect one (*eklectê*) of her that conceived her. The daughters saw her and shall bless (*makariousin*) her; yea, the queens and the concubines and they shall praise her (LXX Song of Songs 6:9)[137]

---

[137] Mary is associated as the dove of God the moment she first enters the Temple at three years old in *Protoevangelium*, 8.2.

133

Mary shall be lauded by future generations of women as blessed due to her elect status in her conception, from her mother's womb, as undefiled. Of course, we can now see why the Protevangelium of the first century recounts Mary's life as an only child from and as someone holy from her mother's womb. Now, we want to know for a twelve-year old girl what: "[The] mighty [one] did great things for me" means. We have found this exact phraseology in Job 5:8-11, Psalm 135:4-5, and Sirach 50:22.[138] Of course, there is a common theme. First, for Job, God does mighty or inexplicable things when he makes dew fall upon earth (fertilization theme) and as waters come up from their springs (origins theme). Secondly, the Psalmist sees God's mighty works as the creation of the heavens and the waters above the heavens, and finally, Sirach who fills out the mystery: "He hath done great things (*ton megala poiounta*) in all the earth who raises our days from our mothers' womb (*ton hypsounta hêmeras êmôn ek mêtras*)." The mighty works that God did for Mary concentrate on her creation and her endowment with the virtue humility from her mother's womb. As such, she merited to be called Sirach's singular: "someone full of grace." She produced both a good gift and word without defilement (Sirach 18:15-17). Now we have come full circle to the Annunciation, where Gabriel recognizes her as the fulfillment of this human paradigm of virtue even before their conversation.

Continuing on, the term by Mary and Sirach: "raise/raising" (*hypsounta*), is not specific (Sirach 50:22-24). There are two main uses in the relevant Old Testament texts. Rev. Dr. Brown is right to report that the primary figurative meaning in this context is to raise the oppressed or humbled poor. One of Luke's principal sources supplying him Greek vocabulary to reformulate Hannah's hymn is Sirach. Sirach makes it clear that one may be born humble in utero but

---

[138] Brown, *The Birth of the Messiah*, 358, 361, admirably notices the connection between Genesis 18:14: "nothing is too wonderful/beyond the power (*adynaton*) of God" and Mary's "The one who is powerful (*dynatos*)" who did great things for Mary. However, Genesis 18:14 refers to God's wonders that are his creation of children (not principally delivering the Egyptians). When God mentions Israel's deliverance Genesis 18:14 matches the Hebrew vocabulary of the miracles by which God delivered them (whether creations or intervention), as for example the miracle of the Red Sea. Brown refers to LXX Deuteronomy 10:21, as a valid verse grounding Mary's embrace of this principle: God first claims that the earth and heaven belong to him (10:14), then that he elected a seed –saving it by his wonders– to be multiplied over the earth. The merit of Brown's passage is that it also includes care for the widow and the orphan, and alien, not dissimilar from the oppressed mentioned by Hannah and the humble by Mary.

nonetheless can be lifted up by God by an act of mercy, granting "joyfulness" (*euphrosynê*) to the humble one. This of course is exactly the theme in Mary's song! She was conceived as the Lord's blameless or perfect dove in the womb, humble (by the creative operations of God) and God raised her up from that moment by an act of mercy so that she can say to Elizabeth that she had a miraculous joy sometime in the past that places her on a throne (of David) above her fellows.

While we have already dealt with Luke 1:51, with regard to the proud, since Mary refers to herself oppositely as a humble servant, we have nonetheless to explain the phrase: "He has shown strength with his arm" (*kratos* [=*keras*]). Again, Sirach 47:5 refers to this as a phrase that is explicitly an alternative way of expressing Hannah's notion of "lifting up/exalting my horn." For Sirach, it is God who lifts up his arm for David against some external threat, whereby the power or horn of God's chosen people is exalted. It is curious that Mary does not wish to mention the "horn" though Hannah does at the beginning and at the end of her hymn. Hannah mentions the exalted horn with respect to her victory over her detractors by her conception and ends mentioning the messiah's future victory over his enemies as somehow related to her pregnancy of Samuel. In the New Testament we saw that Zachariah refers to Hannah's language of a horn being lifted up with respect to the forthcoming birth of Christ, but why does Mary emphasize the strong arm over and above mention of the horn? I think it likely that the theme from Sirach reveals her motivations: Mary has been emphasizing during her hymn that she is of the house of David. Hence, some of her reformatting of Hannah's hymn is to accommodate her identity as a daughter of the olden messiah, King David, and to concentrate on the marvels God has done for her prior to the conception of Jesus.

Luke 1:52-54: "He has put down the mighty from their thrones and exalted the lowly-humble. He has filled (*eneplêsen*) the hungry with good things and the rich he has sent away empty (compare 1 Samuel 2:10; Genesis 31:41-42; Deuteronomy 15:12-13). Mary's hymn is clearly rearranging Hannah's interesting linkage between oppression of the afflicted, poor, sterile or so-called humble and God's providential giving life and distributing death. We discover a giant chiasmus in Hannah (1 Samuel 2:5-7):

A_1: Exalting Hannah's horn

135

B₁: Lord's holiness and justice

C₁: Warning against pride

D₁: He weakens the powerful and strengthens the weak

E₁: God fills (*plêreis*) hungry and weakens powerful for he makes the sterile fertile

and the mother of many feeble

F: The Lord gives death and bring life; he brings down to Hades and raises up

E₂: God makes rich and poor; he humbles and exalts (*tapeinoi kai anypsoi*)

D₂: He blesses with freedom the just man by removing him from the powerfuls' grasp

C₂: Warnings against pride

B₂: The messiah's justice in judging on behalf of the lowly-poor

A₂: Exalting messiah's horn

Mary's hymn, as Rev. Dr. Brown's ecumenical scholarly team agree, *is not about Jesus and Mary*. It is about Mary's status in Luke's mind![139] She is the humble daughter of David whose horn is not exalted in the sense of Hannah, for Mary ought not to have had many children by now. When Mary identifies herself as "God's slave" and her opponents as the one's "sent away empty," she seems to allude to Genesis 31:41-42 and Deuteronomy 15:12-13, as unjust cases of powerful and rich persons like Laban sending away virtuous and poor slaves such as Patriarch Jacob. The Deuteronomistic legislation on this point can be read by its phraseology and vocabulary to be an attempt to put a stop to the evil of sending a slave away, just as Laban famously did with Jacob, attempting to deny Jacob even his wife and children. For Mary, as Ark of the Covenant, sending her away empty

---

[139] Brown, *Mary in the New Testament*, 141.

leads to a curse and destruction of any populace or city who would dare send the Ark away (*eksapostellousin*) empty (*kenên*) or without gifts offered in honor of her to please God and to make a propitiation (*eksilastêrion*) for sin ([LXX=] 1 Samuel 5:10-6:4). Mary's age (twelve or fourteen) would coincide with the fourteen years of Patriarch Jacob's service to Laban and double the Israelite six-year slavery law (or double the release-date of slaves in the seventh year of servitude). Mary was either twelve or fourteen at the Annunciation and she received her just wage for her years of servitude to God. It is attractive to see the numerology of twelve or fourteen in Jacob or the Levitical slave-law years being a kind of type to be fulfilled in Mary's service to God prior to her Annunciation. Notice that Hannah's hymn does not centralize liberation theology as such but rather the central point of the chiasmus argues that the Lord mysteriously creates death and gives life in the womb to whom he will. The central connections between hungry people and Mary's hymn lies in their being "filled" upon God predetermining who shall be poor, determining to whom he shall give life in the womb, and to whom he shall make sterile. These themes, like Hannah's hymn, are clearly picked up by Luke 1:51: "[He] exalted the lowly-humble (*hypsôsen tapeinous*)." Mary is humble from her mother's womb and was lifted up. God long ago "filled" Hannah with a child, just as God "fills" miraculously stomachs with food of formerly hungry people; so that both are "filled." The central theme of Mary's mention of the poor is being filled and concerns God who shall bring about the death of proud lineages of Israel in a Mary as one who "filled" (her own sterile mother's womb[?]) just as Elizabeth was "filled" with the Spirit by divine providence with the embryonic Baptist present. If on the other hand Mary's filling alludes to Jesus, then God shall raise up this humble child Jesus from Hades –like Hannah's hymn– (which is an anticipation of Resurrection), namely, the messiah from Sheol.

As we can see, Mary's reformulation of Hannah's hymn retains the mention of "filling." This is not arbitrary, nor primarily social-justice oriented, since the beginning of Elizabeth's introduction [above A_1] and the end of the Magnificat chiasmus [above A_2] both speak of "filling." Hence, we see both Hannah and Mary referring to being filled with food, which is clearly a metaphor to imagine an empty womb being filled and a fertile womb going empty without any more children. Empty or full stomachs of people are at God's mysterious choice and the justice of that choice is hardly evident to us. It is true, as Rev. Dr. Brown asserts, that a theology of liberation of the poor is very much to the forefront during Hannah's time by looking to God, or at least during the time of publishing

Hannah's hymn by its redactor. For her part, Mary adopts the metaphor primarily for stylistic reasons and its associations with pregnancy.

Luke 1:55: "He has helped his child Israel, in remembrance of his mercy, as he spoke to our fathers, to Abraham and to his seed forever." Sirach 50:23, one of the two main sources for Mary's vocabulary and phraseology in her hymn, affirms an eschatological dimension to her marvelous creation as a virtuous daughter of David, and God's dove or perfect, namely, Mary is meant to bear the "seed" or "offspring" of Abraham, Isaac, and Jacob, whose lineage became the twelve tribes. This lineage, conserved in faithful Judah, represents all Israelites awaiting their messiah. The child Israel is literally the promise extended to the patriarch, but also figuratively a community of believers identified by the name of Jacob, and it is even eschatologically or in the end times identifying the christ or messiah who shall come from this lineage through Mary as the (First and the) Last (child, offspring, only begotten, single claimant to the Davidid dynasty).

When we have used the principle of interpreting Scripture by Scripture's own sources, we arrive at intricate and convincing arguments to support the foregoing findings about Mary in the New Testament. Our theology is guided by trusting the Evangelists selection of Scriptural passages and we are faithful to Luke's sources. This pays large dividends in what is often advertised as a poor economy for capitalizing on Marian doctrine. Quite the opposite, interpreting Scripture by Scripture or Luke by his own sources justifies early Christian readings of Mary's vocation and privileges. Unexpectedly, Sirach suggests that Mary's humility and her title "Full of Grace" should be thought to be a call from the womb. Luke himself unmistakably reworks Sirach chapters 18 and 50. As an author, Luke might be taking liberties to edit Mary's original Aramaic or local dialectical witness. If she had been a primary and living witness for Luke's narrative, she would have likely cited from her memory of Aramaic Targums read to her, or perhaps from Hebrew hymns known to her and adapted into her own song. Luke would have felt free to adjust her hymn in harmony with translations of Scripture in Greek, since he would have been unable to do the scholarly work of sifting through the Aramaic or Hebrew texts alluded to in Mary's hymn. The net result is that Luke makes Mary into the New Ark, the Daughter of Jephthah, the New Mother of Samson, the New Mother of Samuel, and even the New Man full of grace (Sirach 18:17); she who from her own mother's womb possessed original justice or justification and was free of Eve's curse in order to prepare her to hear the word of God and believe it at the Annunciation and conceive it in both her heart and more literally in her womb.

4.2 The Purification of Mary in Luke 2:22

For the purposes of our investigation, namely, to clear up the most complicated or difficult passages concerning Mary in the New Testament, the mystery of Jesus and Mary's purification in the Temple has yet to be definitively solved by compiling all the Biblical and patristic evidence. The issue stems from the following verse:

> **Luke 2:22:** "When the time was completed for *their* purification" according to the rites required by the Law of Moses (LXX Leviticus 12:6a), Joseph and Mary took him to Jerusalem to present him to the Lord [23] (as it is written in the Law of the Lord, "Every firstborn male is holy who opens the womb shall be called holy (*hagion*) to the Lord" (LXX Exodus 13:2; Judges 13),[24] and to offer a sacrifice in keeping with what is said in the Law of the Lord: "a pair of doves or two young pigeons" (LXX Leviticus 12:8).

Let us notice the intriguing way the Mosaic law was interpreted in Greek and then interpreted by Luke:

LXX Leviticus 12:6a	Luke 2:22a
And when the time was fulfilled of her purification for her son (*kai **hotan** anaplêrôthôsin **hai hêmerai katharseôs autês eph'hiôi**).	And when the time was completed for their purification (*kai **hote** eplêsthêsan **hai hêmerai katharismou** **aὐtῶn**).

Luke's phrase: "for their purification" instead of Exodus saying only "her purification for her son," or "her purification in the matter of law regarding her son," requires of the Greek reader familiarity with the actual application of the written law by its practitioners at the time of translating Exodus into Greek. For his part, Luke makes the interesting connection between Leviticus 12:6 and

139

Exodus 13:2. The point of emphasis for Luke is Exodus. While substantially correct in his translation of Exodus, Luke does not cite Exodus verbatim that reads: "hallow (*hagiason*) to me your firstborn only begotten son." Instead, Luke notes that the result of such a dedication or hallowing is that the firstborn son becomes "holy" (*hagion*). This is linked to Luke's earlier emphasis on the prophecy by Gabriel about the child's identity who shall be "born holy" (Luke 1:35). Recall, the one "born holy" is the "son of God" (Hebrew: *ben Elohim*) who is "hallowed" from the womb in Judges chapter 13, that is, Samson! The theological point here is stunning: The firstborn of Exodus that belongs to God is killed by the Angel of the Lord unless his house is covered in the blood of the lamb. Now, the blood-covered firstborn is similar to Samson, holy from the womb, whose father offers a holocaust of a goat to God and the Angel of the Lord leaps into the holocaust after making himself known as cause of Samson's miraculous conception and then the Angel of the Lord becomes a sacrifice ordinarily offered by the Nazarite family to God. Finally, we see that the Levitical law is a shadowy anticipation that the Angel of the Lord who shall be a firstborn only-begotten of his mother, just as Mary who is offering a holocaust (foreshadowing her son's offering). This human holocaust shall free Israel from its enemy (sin) by the killing of himself (that is, Jesus handing himself over to his passion and death, just as Samson prayed to be allowed to do the same to save Israel from the Philistines when killing them all while yet in chains).

Luke's root word for his term "purification" (*katharismos*) is used exclusively (Luke 2:22; 5:12-14; 7:22; 11:39; 11:41) in a non-moral and purely ritualistic manner of the Mosaic law (as stated in Luke 22:22b explicitly). Greek Leviticus's "purification" (*katharsis*) is unique to Leviticus only. It's original Hebrew (MT Leviticus 12:6a) is טָהֳרָה (*tahorah*). This is used like Luke's Gospel, for priestly, leper, and birth cleansings. Luke 2:22 translates, plausibly according to exegetes, Leviticus 12:6a to implicate Jesus in the holocaust sacrifice. Luke takes the "*eph 'hiôi*" to mean "for" as causal or purpose: "for her son." Mary avoids presenting the "holocaust" sacrifice (the perfect sacrifice and highest offering without implication of sin) in Leviticus 12:6. Instead, she opts for the two doves, one associated with Jesus and one with herself per Luke. Luke's choice is puzzling, for Mary should have ideally bought the perfect sacrifice of a holocaust as prescribed (if possible) for Israelites in Leviticus 12:6. She should have offered the sacrifice according to a strict reading only for herself. Instead, she opts for the poor's sacrifice (perhaps because of her play on words, as one of God's lowly-humble ones in her Magnificat). If, according to Leviticus 12:8, the holocaust-dove

140

can be the perfect sacrifice, then this is clearly symbolizing Jesus's sacrifice as the holocaust. We notice, however, that Mary's Magnificat quotes a reference to herself as being called blessed by all generations (*makariousin*; just like Elizabeth's blessing upon her). There, we noticed that an oblique citation is made as follows: "My dove (*peristera*), my undefiled/blameless (*teleia* [= Hebrew: *tām*]) is but one" (Song of Songs 6:9). It is difficult to avoid the impression that the citation by Luke from Leviticus 12:6 emphasizes that the two animals of purification offering are "doves" (*peristerôn*) (Compare LXX Leviticus 12:8). One can easily infer that both Jesus and Mary are referred to as two perfect or blameless doves who share the exact same biological flesh and who offer this to Yahweh!

Yet, what of the second sacrifice as a propitiation "looking toward sin" (*peri tês hamartias*)? The meaning as rendered by the LXX makes it possible that "the end for the sake of which" the propitiation is offered is "communal sin." Scholars already agree that *nothing in the Mosaic Law* makes it possible to attribute *personal sin to the woman* in this ritual purification; the overtones of this kind of sacrifice make it an attractive hypothesis, but it finds no justification in Scripture. We can only say that Jesus has offered a perfect holocaust and Mary her own propitiation that looks to blot out communal sin. The verb here "propitiate" (*eksilasetai*) fits perfectly Luke's theme in chapters 1-2, 18; namely, the Ark of the Covenant, to which –when gifts are offered it– it becomes a propitiation of sin. Here, Mary offers a gift in relation to her own flesh being associated with the newborn Jesus as a propitiation for sin of the community. The LXX merely states that "the priest will propitiate with her in mind" or "in regard to her" (*peri autês*). The effect of the priest offering the propitiation is that she "will afterwards be ritually cleansed" (*katharisthêsetai*) (Leviticus 12:8) or complete the ceremony of the Mosaic Law. Exegetes note that Luke likely changes the purification into "a family affair" or into a "communal action." This can also account for how the Epistle to the Hebrews interprets Jesus's Mosaic designation as the **firstborn** dedicated to God:

> **Hebrews 12:22**: But you have come to Mount Zion, to the city of the living God, the heavenly Jerusalem. You have come to thousands upon thousands of angels in joyful assembly, [23] to **the church of the firstborn**, whose names are written in heaven. You have come to God, the Judge of all, to the spirits of the righteous made perfect, [24] to Jesus the mediator of a new covenant, and to the sprinkled blood that speaks a better word than the blood of

141

Abel. [...] [28] Therefore, since we are receiving a kingdom that cannot be shaken, let us be thankful, and so worship God acceptably with reverence and awe, [29] for our "God is a consuming fire."

The God, who is a consuming fire, consumes Jesus's holocaust just as Jesus shall be holocaust for Israel. Secondly, Zion is the place of this new church, where angels are with him. The shedding of blood has established this Church. The firstborn and his circumcision cannot be excluded, even if the more obvious and overriding theme will be Jesus's crucifixion. This may simply be an admission that communal worship of the "family of God" began at the establishment of the New Testament church by the hallowing of Jesus by his mother and their conjoint presentation of himself as symbolic holocaust in linkage with the propitiatory offering of Mary, her flesh for the incarnation. This initiates a new form of worship whereby the formerly unsolvable mystery of propitiation attached to purification of a new mother in the Temple is finally solved for scholars of the Mosaic Law. Mary's flesh provides the new holocaust of the ensouled and divine Jesus as she is the principal material source for sacrifice or its *archê*. What cannot be denied is that both Jesus and Mary are associated together as the subjects of purification in these rites. The net result is that the rites are transformed and fulfilled by two agents.

Finally, if Mary's offering of her flesh, as Ark of the Covenant (as in previous chapters), is an important theme for the nativity of Jesus, does it have practical application in Luke's Gospel? Interestingly, the life of prayer is where it applies! Luke applies Mary's identity to the rule of prayer and its value later when recounting the story of the Pharisee and humble tax collector:

Two men went up into the Temple [...] The Pharisee stood **praying to himself [in his heart]**: "O God, I thank you that I am not like others [...] as this tax collector [...] I always tithe from as much [riches] as I own. Now, the tax collector stood afar off. He did not wish to raise his eyes unto heaven but struck **his breast, saying [in his heart]**: "O God, be merciful (*hilasthêti*) to me the sinner.'[140] I tell you, this one went down [from the Temple]

---

[140] Exegetes notice the *hapax legomenon* (*hilasthêti*) of the New Testament is fulfilled in Lk 23:48: after a centurion declares Jesus innocent, then the crowds respond by

142

justified (*deikaiômenos*) [...] because each **who exalts himself**
(*ho hupsôn heauton*), will be humbled (*tapeinôthêsetai*), but he
who humbles himself will be exalted. (Luke 18:10-14)

Luke applies Mary's Magnificat (during Jesus' embryonic life in utero of Mary)
to Jesus's adult saying and parable by using Mary's prophetic liturgical hymn, its
vocabulary, and phraseology, as Jesus's very paradigm for explaining acceptable
Temple worship. Mary exemplifies an acceptable "thanks/eucharist" to God. Now,
the tax collector is asking for forgiveness "at the Mercy Seat of the Ark" in the
Temple. The tax collector says before the place of the Mercy Seat: "Be propitious"
or "*hilasthêti*" before the place where the Ark (now missing should be). What is
happening here? If we turn to Luke's source for Ark language, then we see that the
tax collector takes refuge in the propitiation of the Ark of the Covenant. Turning
to 1 Samuel 5 (= LXX) we find the following:

> The hand of the Lord came against the city [...] They **sent out**
> (*eksapostellousin*) the Ark of God [...] so that it entered into
> Askalon and they cried aloud [...] Send out the Ark of God to
> Israel [...] and it went down unto its place [...] and a cry arose in
> the city toward heaven [...] Certainly, do not send the Ark out
> **empty** (*kenên*) [...] then you will be healed, and [sin] **will be
> propitiated** (*eksilasthêsetai*) [...] For what do you weigh your
> hearts down, as Egypt and Pharaoh weighed down their heart?

Notice that Mary's hymn in Luke chapter 1 or Magnificat is about those sent away
empty like Pharaoh's people at the Exodus of Israel from Egypt (reversing the
fortune of former Hebrew slaves). Also, the notions of crying aloud and shouting
could be the same kind of activity associated with the reception of Jesus with
overshadowing branches in Jerusalem (Palm Sunday). More importantly, it is gifts

---

finally "beating their breasts." In this scene the women and true disciples appear "at a
distance" but not beating their breasts, presumably because they are already "just" or
"justified" at the Mercy Seat of the Cross. The Evangelist reechoes Paul (Romans 3:25)
and Heb 9:5 referring to the cross as the mercy seat (*hilastêrion*) of redemption. The LXX
contains only three such imperatives: (a.) from a prayer for mercy in a liturgical hymn to
the divine name (Ezrah 4:17), (b.) from a prayer of forgiveness in an epiclesis of "the name
of glory" (LXX Psalm 79:9), and (c.) from prayer calling on the divine name in by
Theodotion's translation: "Make this [...] o my God, since your name has been called upon
the city and upon the people" (LXX Dan 9:19).

and offerings left with the Ark that are a propitiation acceptable to God. The inference possible in Luke's Gospel is that the Ark of the Covenant (viz., Mary) in chapter 1 is our propitiation as sinners (just like Luke 2:22), as with the tax collector in Luke chapter 18. Prayer in front of the place (though physically now empty) where the Ark should be, for it has arisen into the heavens like the Psalmist sings (Psalm 132:8-10), is able to obtain reconciliation, peace, and divine favor. The inference made from this is to offer gifts to Mary of prayer, to the risen Ark, to please Yahweh who rested on her, his Mercy Seat, from the time of the Incarnation (Luke 1:35).

4.3 An Excursus into John's Gospel: The Wedding at Cana John 2:4-5

So far, we have concentrated the majority of our studies on Luke's Gospel. Yet, to finish out our study, there is an oft-quoted Johannine passage that is puzzling since it's not clear without any in-depth investigation that we should think of Mary as an unequivocal support to Jesus's public ministry. When it comes to Mary in the Bible, Bible-based Christians sometimes feel historical Christian churches (Roman Catholics, Eastern Orthodox, Oriental Orthodox) are always praising Mary but don't seem to have much helpful to explain such troubling passages of Scripture, which to twentieth-century eyes, look to put Mary in her place for being –at the very least– less than perfect. It is rather foolish to dismiss *Sola Scriptura* or Bible-alone based Christianity on this score because sometimes historical Christianity does not really make any obvious efforts to engage the literal texts of the Scriptures verbatim or at least to try to show how Scripture interprets Scripture in favor of historical Christianity. This results in an understandable suspicion by Bible-alone Christians since a lot of "traditions" seems to be superadded onto Bible reading, but these same traditions don't seem to help much with the literal meaning of the text (even if for most Christians this is always in their modern-day-translation-alone reading, since Greek is a real challenge to learn!). Let us take a look at yet another passage where Mary seems, in 20th century English, to be possibly corrected for imprudence by the God-man Jesus: "When the wine was gone, Jesus' mother said to him, 'They have no more wine.' 'Woman, **what is it between you and me** (*ti emoi kai soi, o gynai*) ?' Jesus replied. 'My hour has not yet come.'" (John 2:3-4)

This study is in the line with our previous investigations on Luke 11:27-28. Mary is sometimes misjudged by English-speaking Christians to get a correction by Jesus; whereas the real message for Bible-alone and historical Christians has been demonstrated in Luke to be the following: Mary was first to hear the word of God and completely keep it. Like about eighty-ninety percent of New Testament, John's citations are from the Greek Old Testament. But let us address some good instincts by English-speaking Bible-alone Christians that are spot-on that make their interpretation of this passage: "What is it between you and me," entirely understandable. Does not this sound like a disagreement? In fact, in the Old Testament and the New Testament it *normally* means a fight, even if one big exception shall prove the rule that will be so very important for us to understand John 2:4. Let us start with what every Bible-alone Christian who knows this saying gets ninety percent of the time correct: This phrase is used for enemies! Let us list every known instance of this phrase in the Greek language outside of the Masoretic text's first Book of Kings:

> Then Jephthah sent messengers to the Ammonite king with the question: "**What** is **between you and me** (*ti emoi kai soi*) that you have attacked my country?" (LXX Judges 11:12).

> But Necho sent messengers to him, saying, "**What** [quarrel] is there, o king of Judah, **between you and me** (*ti emoi kai soi*)? It is not you I am attacking at this time, but the house with which I am at war. God has told me to hurry; so stop opposing God, who is with me, or he will destroy you." (LXX 2 Chronicles 35:21)

> And after each act by Josiah of this kind, it happened that Pharaoh the king came to raise ware in Charkamu on the Euphrates, and he came out for a response to one under Josiah and the king of Egypt sent to that one someone; he said to him: "**What is it between you and me, o king of Judah** (*ti emoi kai soi, o Basileu Ioudaias*)?" (LXX Ezra 1:24)

145

He shouted at the top of his voice, "**What** [is it] **between you and me, o Jesus** (*ti emoi kai soi, o Iēsou*) Son of the Most High God? In God's name don't torture me!" (Mark 5:7)

So aren't you yourself accustomed to say to a person: "**What is it between you and me, o man** (*ti emoi kai soi, anthrôpe*)? Are not my own evils enough for me?" And you speak well, for your own evils are enough for you [why concern yourself over those of others?]. (Epictetus, Dissertations, 2.19.19)[141]

Notice, John 2:4 is one of the rare several passages in all of Greek literature with the phrase: "**What is it between you and me?**" Without yet looking at our key passage –the exception to the rule– it looks like Jesus and Mary did not have domestic bliss. In fact, Jesus appears rather miffed at his mom and is using passages that in Hebrew or Greek (and presumably Aramaic), clearly mean: "**Why are you starting a fight between us?**" Also, notice that in almost all passages, the "**O person 'x'**" follows. First, I ask the question, then I address the person by name: "**o king**," "**o man**" "**o Jesus**." John 2:4 is the same: "**o woman**."

Now, among my citations, why do I even care about Epictetus? Well, Paul cites the same exact rhetorician and his vocabulary as Epictetus does when composing Galatians and Romans! Paul was trained in rhetoric at the Stoic school of Tarsus. This school was founded by Athenodorus of Tarsus who also trained and inspired the court philosopher of Emperor Augustus in Rome, which connects St. Paul's founder of his rhetorical school in Tarsus with Epictetus's rhetoric teacher in Rome, since Athenodorus was the direct inspiration for both. However, elsewhere in his lectures, Epictetus admits to constantly conversing with Jewish philosophers and this saying –believe it or not– is exclusive to Jews in Greek! Epictetus is likely showing that he has absorbed Roman Jewish wisdom (possibly even Christian sayings since Epictetus mentions their use of baptism in his lectures!) in typical Stoic fashion whereby they adopt all wisdom that is true. Here, we have the closest saying to Jesus in the New Testament. Matthew 6:34 is the very same saying that Jesus cites as Jewish wisdom: "Today's evil is enough [why

---

[141] This is the same saying as Jesus knew from the Jews in Matthew 6:34.

worry about another day with all we have to worry about today?]." However, Epictetus knows this Jesus/Jewish wisdom phrase combined with question: "**Why is there fight between you me** [...] don't we have enough evil without our fighting?" Notice, Epictetus shouts: "o man." This is key, for Jesus, likewise shouts: "o woman." Wow! This looks grim for traditional or historical Christians who want to hold onto the idea that Mary is only honored and never rebuked for bad behavior in the New Testament. For now, I agree, every instance we've seen includes: (1.) **A disagreement between two persons**, (2.) **a subsequent fight**, (3.) **the invocation of the person's name who is the adversary** *not a friend*!

Using the principle of Scripture interpreting Scripture, we must try to understand what Jesus's experience at the wedding of Cana with his first public miracle is supposed to accomplish. What is he signifying, what is he teaching, what role does Mary play in the realization of Jesus's prophetic, messianic, and divine mission? Well, let us take a look at what the author John is doing when he adjusts the Aramaic or (less likely) local Hebrew conversations and translates them by carefully referring to the language and type of Jesus in the Old Testament, namely, Elijah:

(LXX =) 1 Kings 17:7-24	John 2:2-12
7 Sometime later the brook dried up because there had been no rain in the land. 8 Then the word of the Lord came to him: 9 "Go at once to Zarephath in the region of Sidon and stay there. I have directed a <u>widow</u> there to supply you with food." 10 So he went to Zarephath. When he came to the town gate, a widow was there gathering sticks. He called to her and asked, "Would you bring me **a little water in a jar** so I may have a drink?" 11 As she was going to get it, he called, "And bring me, please, a piece of bread." 12 "As surely as the Lord your God lives," she replied, "I don't have any bread—only a handful of flour in	2 On the third day a wedding took place at Cana in Galilee. Jesus' mother was there, and Jesus and his disciples had also been invited to the <u>wedding</u>.[3] When the wine was gone, Jesus' mother said to him, "They have no more wine." "**Woman, why do you involve me, o woman** (*ti emoi kai soi, gynai*)?" Jesus replied. "My hour has not yet come." [5] His mother said to the servants, "Do whatever he tells you." [6]Nearby stood <u>six stone water jars</u>, the kind used by the Jews for ceremonial washing, each holding from twenty to thirty gallons. [7] Jesus said to the servants, "*Fill the jars with water*"; so they filled them to the brim. [8] Then he told them, "Now draw

a jar and a little olive **oil in a jug**. [...] we may eat it—and die." 13 Elijah said to her, "Don't be afraid. Go home and do as you have said. But first make a small loaf of bread for me from what you have and bring it to me, and then make something for yourself and your son. 14 *For this is what the Lord, the God of Israel, says: 'The jar of flour will not be used up and the jug of oil will not run dry until the day* the Lord sends rain on the land.'" 15 She went away and did as Elijah had told her. So there was food every day for Elijah and for the woman and her family. 16 For the jar of flour was not used up and the *jug* **of oil** did not run dry, in keeping with the word of the Lord spoken by Elijah. 17 Sometime later the son of the woman who owned the house became ill. He grew worse and worse, and finally stopped breathing. 18 She said to Elijah, "**What [do you have against] me and you, o man** (*ti emoi kai soi, anthrôpe*) of God? Did you come to remind me of my sin and kill my son?" ¹⁹ "Give me your son," Elijah replied. He took him from her arms, carried him to the upper room where he was staying, and laid him on his bed. ²⁰ Then he cried out to the Lord, *"Lord my God, have you brought tragedy even on this widow I am staying with, by causing her son to die?"* ²¹ Then he stretched himself out on the boy three times and cried out to the Lord, "Lord my God, let this boy's

some out and take it to the master of the banquet." They did so, ⁹ and the master of the banquet tasted the water that had been turned into wine. He did not realize where it had come from, though the servants who had drawn the water knew. Then he called the bridegroom aside ¹⁰ and said, "Everyone brings out the choice wine first and then the cheaper wine after the guests have had too much to drink; but you have saved the best till now."¹¹ What Jesus did here in Cana of Galilee was the first of the signs through which he revealed his glory; and his disciples believed in him. ¹² After this he went down to Capernaum with his mother and brothers and his disciples. There they stayed for a few days.

life return to him!" [22] The Lord heard Elijah's cry, and the boy's life returned to him, and he lived. 23 Elijah picked up the child and carried him down from the room into the house. He gave him to his mother and said, "Look, your son is alive!" [24] *Then the woman said to Elijah, "Now I know that you are a man of God and that the word of the Lord from your mouth is the truth*."

The mystery is solved! John writes his Gospel conscientious that Elijah (who was raised into heaven on God's chariot where only God typically drives) was meant to be an imperfect anticipation of Jesus. Both raised the dead, the miracle most symbolic of God's power to give life.

Notice the reasons why John the Evangelist is careful to refer obliquely to 1 Kings 17: Mary is likely, by now a widow (since Joseph never is mentioned to follow him), while the widow known to Elijah also has many children whom she looks after. This is not dissimilar from the tradition that Joseph had a family or children prior to marrying Mary (even if this is ultimately not that important). The point is that Mary and the widow are the same and that both have a child who will die and who will be raised in the context of the sacred number three: Jesus in three days, the widow's boy by three ceremonial acts. Both see the setting for the encounter with a person called: "woman," to include some occasion to drink water. However, in both cases, the real miracle is not the water but occasioned by it. For Elijah, this is the moment where he multiplies a container of oil (and flour), while for Jesus the water is the occasion to change its very essence or nature into something healthful and joy-filled for mankind; namely, wine. Elijah is facing a national crisis of unbelief and unfaithfulness leading to the destruction of Israel, where only a widow outside the border of Israel is his ally; whereas Jesus is not in at a funeral or with a widow but at a wedding, where he is preparing to celebrate the restoration of true kingship to Israel within its borders. Elijah had to flee East of the Jordan to be served by the widow, while Jesus's wedding takes place well within Israel's borders and is a sign of restoration and celebration. Elijah's miracle is private to one just woman, but the wedding feast miracle is public to manifest by a public woman the change in the fortunes of Israel back to faithfulness.

So, in this context, notice the exact nature of the just widow's question to Elijah: **"What is it between you and me, o man of God?"** She is afraid that her son dying is a punishment of sin that is delivered upon the head of her boy. Instead, Elijah demonstrates that the opposite is true; she is not an unjust woman but the coming of Elijah has nonetheless seemingly brought tragedy to her household by her son dying. He prays that she should see that this is *not the case*! In the old Testament type and the New Testament fulfillment, the woman is the occasion for the man of God (whether Elijah or Jesus) to perform a miracle. The woman in both instances does not understand the larger picture of the holy man's destiny or prechosen lot by divine will; but in both cases the woman is only seemingly at odds with the holy man. In the first instance, Elijah shows her that she is not sinful and does not deserve a dead son, and in the second instance Jesus uses this very phrase and reverses it to illustrate a similar point; namely, that Mary's orders are already within the plan of God for Jesus's manifestation to Israel. With Elijah, when the widow cried out "o man (of God)," it was adversarial but not indicative of the prophet being thought of by her as sinful but only problematic because the widow thought God justly to punish her or to have something against her. Likewise, Jesus cries out "o woman (of God)," who is only apparently against the will of God by asking him to do his first public miracle on her own volition. Since "woman of God" is not Biblical, we cannot expect John to use a phrase "woman of God." Typically "woman" is left to stand on its own since this is how God and Adam address the prototypical woman, Eve. Mary does not know that the wedding-miracle is coming and that it is not *primarily* due to her wishes but *primarily* divine intention, all along, to introduce Jesus publicly by a wedding feast as the savior of Israel (a wedding, not funeral!) to bring back faithfulness to God and to cause belief among Israelites in his divine mission. In both cases, the woman widow and the woman Mary are unwittingly and only superficially pitted against the greater divine plan of the holy man: the widow by her **"what is it...o man"** and Jesus by his **"what is it...o woman."** In reality, they are both occasions for God to manifest his real plan to demonstrate his greatness to the people he means to save from sin and from death. Jesus's "o woman" is reversing the widow's apparent disagreement with Elijah and showing that he and his mother are only *seemingly at odds* but really both want what is according to God's will. Jesus underlines that Mary and he seem on the surface (Like the widow and Elijah) to have different plans, but his subsequent obedience to Mary's plan, like Elijah to the widow,

150

demonstrates a deeper divine plan of two people being allies that lead to the glory of God unfolding in history. The result is that the disciples (in the Gospel) and the widow (in the Old Testament) are brought to believe more strongly in the mission of their respective holy man.

Conclusions

It is entirely understandable that Christians of whatever sort today find in John 2:4 a mystery and worry about Mary's status. Even saints of the past were aware that only an attentive reader of both Old and New Testaments would be able to see the deeper meaning. The best summation of this is St. Romanos the Hymnographer writing in his native Greek around 550 AD:

But Christ seeing His mother saying, "Grant me this request,"

At once said to her: "What do you wish, woman, my hour has not come."

Certain men made use of this saying as a pretext for impiety;

They said that Christ, submitted to necessity,

They said that He was a slave to periods of time. ...

"Now answer, my child," said the all-holy mother of Christ,

"Thou who dost control with measurement the periods of time, how, my son and Lord, dost Thou await a time?

Thou who hast regulated the division of the seasons, how dost thou await a season?

Thou who art the creator of the visible and the invisible,

Thou who, as master, dost day and night regulate

The ceaseless revolutions, as Thou dost will them—

Thou who hast defined the years in beautifully ordered cycles—

How, then, dost Thou await a time for the miracle which I ask of Thee

Who hast in wisdom created all things?"

151

"I knew before you told me, revered Virgin, that the wine was just beginning to give out for them,"

The Ineffable and Merciful straightway answered His holy mother.

"I know all the concerns of your heart which you set in motion in this matter; For within yourself you reasoned as follows: 'Necessity now summons my son to a miracle,

And He puts it off under the pretext of "the time." '

Holy mother, learn now the meaning of the delay,

For when you know it, I shall grant you this favor,

I, who in wisdom have created all things.[142]

And again, the same Romanos writes:

"For if they had understood all these things at the time when they saw the awesome miracles,

They would understand that I am God before time, even though I have become man.

But now, contrary to order, before the teaching, you have asked for miracles;

And it is for this reason that I delayed a short time in answer to you:

If I was waiting for the time to perform miracles,

It was for this reason alone.

But, since it is necessary that parents be honored by their children,

I shall pay observance to you, Mother, for I am able to do all things,

I, who have in wisdom created all things."[143]

---

[142] Romanos the Melodist, *Kontakion on the Marriage at Cana*, in *John 1-10*, ed. J. Elowsky (Downers Grove IL: InterVarsity Press, 2006), 92-93 (7.10-12).

[143] Romanos, *Kontakion on the Marriage at Cana*, 7.12-16.

Jesus could have only obeyed his mother if there was no conflict, if her timely, earthly and good intentions aligned with the divine intention or plan. Only if Mary ordered Jesus to do the will of the Father could Jesus have obeyed. The mystery is how Mary –with limited access to the divine iCloud in the sky– was able to choose what had already been planned; this is the mystery of how grace can influence Mary's choice even when her knowledge of God's providence is not complete, for she is a mere creature.

So what does John 2:4 prove? What is it that we *must believe* about Mary? Actually, the conclusion is modest: Neither does Jesus rebuke, nor does he grant her any special status that we can discern; rather, he acknowledges that –like her type in Elijah's widow– she has an important historical role in pointing to the mission of the messiah. Jesus is teaching, however, in John's Gospel that apparent contradictions are just that, the deeper meaning of the relationship between Jesus and his mother always needs to be read in light of the role that Mary plays in the history of salvation; namely, she is a compliment and a help to Jesus's ministry and she does not thwart or detract from it. Even if we cannot say that there is anything over the top in either a positive or negative direction of interpretation of this passage, we can conclude that it is a passage that shows the harmony of the Gospels; namely, just as Luke chapters 1-2 and Luke 11:28 clearly testify to the privileged life of grace and holiness of Mary and her promise of perpetual virginity and justification from before the Annunciation, so too John 2:4 is very much concerned with supplementing another vignette of Mary's life with her son Jesus to explain how an historical event of some interest, if not worrisome gossip, about the family of Jesus is actually rooted in Jesus fulfilling his type, Elijah. The worthy and quasi-prophet able to ride on the chariot throne of Yahweh and to made worthy to raise the dead is such by God's permission. In Jesus, no longer passively by the miracle of divine power, but rather actively by his possession and exercise of the Father's power does Jesus transform the essence of natural substances into other substances. In short, Mary's role in John's Gospel is entirely consistent with her role as a heroin in Luke, so that a harmony, not a cacophony, of witnesses speak about the mother of Jesus in the four Gospels.

General Conclusions

This in-depth study of the Evangelists and their teaching about Mary in the New Testament may represent the first systematic investigation into the subject in modern times.[144] The selection of passages, it is true, has mainly been dictated by the general confusion and even controversy that surrounds these well-known verses that touch upon Mary in the Gospels. Although methods used for our investigation are not new, the conclusions shall feel –even to the Marian specialist– entirely new, even revolutionary for reading Scripture.

First, we naturally had recourse to modern historical-critical (source and form criticism) studies that helped us understand the status of the question with respect to each of these passages, whether we speak of Rev. Dr. Brown and his team of scholars, or about more general agreement among scholars from published commentaries on the Old and New Testaments (see the instruments section of the bibliography). While these studies helped us understand what has been written on the topic, it is generally safe to say that specialists do not really show much appreciation for the auxiliary aid of the patristic tradition. So, to these we added a bountiful consultation with mainly Greek, but also Syriac and Latin Fathers.

Next, the patristic tradition itself relied on the allegorical, anagogical, and typological readings of Scripture (not to mention the literal or historical sense of the Bible). For the most part, it is their typological sensitivities that have taught us to root around for many discoveries that we found in a number of cases. Still, systematization of one or two insights within one large tome by an author, in combination with excerpts from other Fathers in a like manner, may appear to be entirely new due principally to the lack of systemization of older arguments and isolated typological claims. We mean that, while a person can hunt and peck to discover in any number of Fathers and Medieval Commentators most, if not all, of our points of interpretation, it would be virtually impossible to find a systematic streamlining and vetting of various interpretations in order to authenticate those that have a basis on the literal sense of Scripture. We mean to say that the literal

---

[144] We distinguish systematic theological study from source-criticism and form-criticism by our additional use of patristics, their exegetical methods, as well as the aforesaid observations of Rev. Dr. Brown et al., altogether employed with and guided by the presumption that a theological set of conclusions can be made from rational harmonization of all the aforesaid.

sense refers to the very syntax, vocabulary, and idioms used by the Evangelists that, by and large, presuppose an in-depth knowledge of the Septuagint and even of some intertestamental literature. If we were to systemize all of the interpretations and validate patristic readings that are based upon a good grammatical, or especially typological, analysis by Fathers of the Church, even this is not enough to account for our readings.

The Fathers practiced a discipline of memorization regarding everywhere a key vocabulary word and phrase were employed and repeated in the Old Testament for comparison of said phrases and terms to the New Testament. The hope was that, like Jewish attentiveness to where and when a word was used in the Hebrew Scriptures, patristic attentiveness would root out prophetic material or insights for the deeper meaning of a term or phrase in the New Testament. Of course, this kind of reading, supposing literary dependence of Evangelists on the Septuagint and its narratives or stories, is admitted by both historical-critical and typological readers of the past. What we have, furthermore, added to our readings are the Jewish concerns for the symbolic or thematic use of a particular terms, or turns of phrase, in the Hebrew Scriptures that were received as prophetic in their overtones, as witnessed in intertestamental or Second Temple literature. For example, the use of the term "wonderful," when we read ancient liturgical texts under Jewish theological influence, leads us to conclude that Judeo-Christians were very sensitive to the Old Testament patterns and application of this particularly messianic vocabulary word throughout the whole of the Old Testament. Our knowledge of the patristic and liturgical interpretations of these Jewish-prophetic traditions greatly aided our ability to understand the typology behind a number of Evangelists' references in this study.

The use of typological readings was invaluable, since their disciplined use shows a respect for Old Testament modes of expression, metaphors, or vocabulary employed by the New Testament writers and typologists. Since the New Testament writers espouse explicitly typology, allegory, and practice anagogy, to ignore Evangelists who are often looking to the Septuagint, or even aspects of the Hebrew, for paradigms and fulfillment of shadows in the New Testament is to neglect both a Biblical and patristic mode of interpretation. It is true of course that typology and allegory, especially the latter, ran so rampant in such an undisciplined manner in the Middle Ages that an instinctive recoil by scholars was understandable in the modern age. However, by ignoring types and by refusing to see how the very Evangelists valued them, much of the New Testament remains opaque. It should especially be noted that much of the modern adversity toward typology springs out of the Reformation rightly noticing a general lack of appreciation for the literal sense. But, it should also be noted that Reformers were reacting, by and large, to Latin authors who were using typological arguments based upon Latin translations of the Bible that were themselves unable to reflect the original wordplays, typological connections, and prophetic readings that a Greek or Hebrew (or Aramaic) version of the texts would have provided. Instead, the Latin authors' game was hit or miss. Sometimes the *Old Latin* (still in use in the High Middle Ages) or Jerome's famous Vulgate was able to support the aforementioned readings or typological and literary dependencies of a New Testament passage on the Old Testament, but oftentimes it was at a lost in translation to justify its claim. Instead, the Latin Christians (and Syriac Christians) had often to rely on their earliest traditions (Liturgy and Pre-Nicene traditions) of Scriptural interpretation where their hymnographers and commentators were often bilingual or very much in touch with a Christian culture that had not abandoned apologetic arguments meant to convert Jews by means of presenting Jewish dialogue-partners with Hebrew Scriptural or Intertestamental literature that admitted a common prophetic meaning between Jews and Judeo-Christians of the first two centuries of our era.

This facet of Jewish-Christian interpretation can be felt most acutely nowadays when search engines like the *Thesaurus Linguae Graecae* and other instruments allow for us to practice a truly disciplined research where we can see both prophetic and typological readings of the Old Testament as embraced by Jews and Christians about the messiah and his rule. When authors like Rev. Dr. Brown were in the midst of their groundbreaking research, they could not logon to a giant database at will, for the most part, nor search nearly replete collections of Greek, Hebrew, and Syriac literature in order to argue for the exclusivity or singularity of readings and interpretations shared between an Evangelist and the Septuagint. This method of investigation can now be performed in a matter of minutes and entire manuscripts can be read in the comfort of one's own home since they are increasingly made available on the internet. Entire collections of patristic literature are also available online, whether in the original language or in translation. The same can be said of Hebrew literature in its various strains, whereby Jewish beliefs about the messiah, as handed on by the New Testament, can be more easily confirmed by access to Second Temple literature. On one hand, this means that the feats of past scholars who relied on memory and concordances is perhaps more impressive than the labor of our study here, in the sense that they did much more with cruder instruments. On the other hand, our work, insofar as we are disciplined

157

and methodologically sound, surpasses modern studies by maximizing our ability to put the entire Greek tradition of literature still extant in dialogue with Greek-Christian writers and even non-Christians who read and interpreted Christian Scriptures. There are many things to be learned from our predecessors and we have benefitted from them greatly but they have sometimes missed obvious connections to the Septuagint as proposed by the Evangelists.

With regard to the method of this study, we have shown that the Synoptics actually provide a fundamentally unified approach to the person and character of Mary in the New Testament. This should hardly be surprising, if indeed they all accepted as a rule the authority of commonly shared source-texts from which they drew their Jesus and Mary stories that could not be supplied by any other means than by this common source. Given disparity with respect to the year of composition, the locale, and the Evangelists' diverse backgrounds, we see that they fundamentally harmonize on the outlook and theological role that Mary plays. The main difference between and among them has more to do with the allowance they make for the inclusion of Jesus's family members in general into the Gospel story out of understandable preoccupation that the saving news for the Israel (and then for the entire world) might be restricted to a family affair monopolized by a rather insignificant Davidic branch of Israel in backwater Galilee. Instead, by and large, the non-genetic leadership of the early Christian community is emphasized in the earlier Evangelists. The Evangelists are often happy to display biological kin who claim to be disciples in the midst of their disagreements. What is more, even our singularly investigated selection from John's Gospel carries on the tradition of typological reading of the Old Testament, common to the four Evangelists, to understand the significance of the unique material in the possession of John about Mary and Jesus.

In each one of these cases, the literary form for a Mary story seems to be prima facie a curious vignette from the life of the family. Instead of being given an idealized or synthesized story, we are presented with very messy and complex data about Mary and her family in most cases under investigation. When we see the Gospel writer offering some theological or spiritual reflections on common or otherwise ambivalent material that could be turned in a negative direction against Mary and her family, then we have no overarching sense that the community invented an idealized story but wrestled with the manner to interpret data presented as brute facts and in need of deeper meaning by a theologian representing the spiritual values of the Evangelist and his community in question. Nonetheless, what does it say that in each and every Evangelist we have discovered whereby Mary was a valued member of Jesus's eschatological family or faith-family awaiting the second coming? The Evangelists may use different nuances to interpret the same ambiguous data about Mary and her family but –whether we call it purely inspiration, or a combination of the Evangelists' human authorial genius and divine inspiration– each Evangelist has taken rough and ready data demanding an explanation due to being historical (viz., an unedited piece of Jesus-history in need of a theological interpretation to confirm it as contributive to Jesus's messiahship). From Mark to Matthew and even to Luke we found obvious, consistent, and surprising evidence that was only available piecemeal in the Septuagint and Fathers about the family structure of Jesus's household. The key to the understanding of Jesus's family lies in the value of the Septuagint for interpreting the source materials used by Mark, Matthew, and Luke. All of them, whether this was in the source materials noticed by their knowledge of Mark's underlying citations or some other explanation, saw that the division of families for census purposes in the Book of Numbers allowing them to tell the story of Jesus's family accurately by using Jewish divisions, even if the writer was not himself from a Jewish background. A marvelous consistency in their application of Numbers allows us to see that the genealogy of Matthew, the stories of Jesus's family in Mark chapters 3 and 6, the infancy narratives in Matthew chapters 1-2 and Luke chapters 1-2, as well as the discussion of Mary's role in Matthew chapter 13 and Luke chapter 11. They all suppose that Jesus is the biological son of Mary alone, the putative son of Joseph, either the half-brother or first cousin to James, Joses, Simon, and Jude, and the distant cousin to his female kin of his patrilineal bloodline by Joseph at his house at Nazareth. We also see that Mary is likely the second wife of Joseph (though leaving room for Joseph's lack of children without a first marriage), and that Mary herself is either the half-sister or first cousin of Elizabeth. We noted that Joseph himself belonged to an extended family unit in Bethlehem, while Mary's relation to her ancestral city seems negligible from information in the Gospels. Finally, we were able to demonstrate Mary's perpetual virginity as taught somewhat obliquely by the infancy narrative of Matthew but explicitly and clearly taught by the infancy narrative of Luke. These discoveries alone are meritorious of a full-length book.

The richness of the Gospel of Luke does not allow us to end there. Building on Mark's and Luke's designation of Mary as, respectively, someone who does God's will and hears God's word and keeps it, Luke expands Mary's honors to place her on a pedestal that is quite surprising for a first-century author. However, our in-depth analysis immediately explains how natural the first or second-century *Protevangelium of James* builds on themes that are intrinsic to Luke's Gospel. The most notable of these themes are Mary's reference to a miraculous experience prior to Elizabeth's conception of St. John the Baptist. To all appearance Mary appeals to God's mighty works at her own creation, as if she is just such a marvel as the heavens or the waters above the heavens. Even if we take the "great things done" for her sake to mean a moral or ethical concern, this still signifies that by, analogy, God created the heavens pure and that they are his possession and so he endowed Mary with analogous moral gifts to conclude that she is the very end term of the movement of history and creation (perhaps this tradition is manifested by the planets and stars orbiting her in Revelation chapter 12). In other words, God made all past marvels in the world by this phraseology purely for Mary's sake. Whichever interpretation is preferred (if not both), it carries the shocking sense in the Greek verbs of the past tense that privileges of Mary are over and above all other human persons in her first days of existence. Mary's honors in Luke are so hyperbolic that we can either suspect that Luke is injecting his personal admiration of a woman either still alive and known to him, or someone whom he is recollecting by recourse to hagiographic saints-lives already circulating about Mary (not unlike the *Protevangelium of James*).

In the end, the Magnificat stands as a monument to Mary's singular vocation and to rhetoric of quasi-excessive praise, as composed by Luke. It is startling that an Evangelist would so early be so preoccupied with the mother of the Redeemer while the church was still very much expecting in some quarters the imminent return of Jesus; since he did not hint at the hour or day prior to his Ascension. To be distracted by the glories of Mary, such that nearly two full chapters of anecdotes and texts are dedicated to her alone, is a sign of the importance that she factually played in the eyes of the first and second generations of Christians and that the ministry she gave to her own son was one notable to followers of Jesus among the crowds.

Our short excursus into John with regard to his only truly problematic Marian passage shows that authentic stories of family interaction fascinated the early communities. The Evangelists either had to address problems arising from these puzzling stories, or to give them a theological justification for retelling since their salvific meaning was not obvious or entirely self-evident for the proclamation of salvation and Resurrection. In some cases the stories served to rebuke Jesus's extended family members who were impeding the Evangelists' contemporary communities from controlling the message about the New Testament kerygma or preaching of the Gospel. If we use these interpretive lenses to account for such stories, then we may wonder if the non-problematic, the devotional, and the pietistic stories about Mary (and other family members) were by and large ignored by the Evangelists. The pious stories of Jesus's family must not have detracted or risked detracting from Jesus's mission or from Mary's honor as virgin begetter of the savior. Furthermore, such hypothetically-pious Mary stories would contain the kinds of facts that would not have risked bolstering Jesus's extended family in opposition to the apostles in their claims to church leadership. Granted this scenario, after the fall of Jerusalem, we predictably see the idiosyncratic addition of newly pious and devotional material by separate Evangelists may signal a change in missiology or strategy by the preaching of the very apostles and disciples after the destruction of the Temple. The new mention of Mary at the foot of the cross, the role of Mary at the Annunciation and Magnificat all signal a change in atmosphere. Still, all Evangelists made sure to include potentially problematic material that expresses the ambivalent position of Jesus's family members. The only efforts to save familial face made by the Evangelists were always to exclude mention of Joseph and Mary from naughty lists and to make sure that something paradigmatic could be mentioned about Mary, or about Mary's and Jesus's cousins who were specifically engaged in ministering to him.

Altogether, even if we are aided by the impressions and teachings and remembrances of later Christians beginning in the second century to direct our search toward particular beliefs (for example, the perpetual virginity and virgin birthing), it is nonetheless true that we can very easily and harmoniously read the Evangelists in agreement on these questions that have traditionally bothered Christians in later centuries, such as the brothers and sisters of Jesus, the perpetual virginity of Mary, and the privileges of Mary over the apostolic community from her creation and time in the womb until her death. In short, by patiently decoding the Evangelists rearrangement of more primitive data to better accord with the sacred language of Septuagint, the Greek translation of their originally Aramaic or Hebrew data was substantially preserved in its content but more clearly linked to its translated Greek point of reference in the Old Testament. Of course, if God had chosen for his own reasons to inspire Evangelists to write in Hebrew or Aramaic, as in the days of old, we would be looking at the same kinds of wordplays, prophecies, and types but these passages would have been immediately disposed for citation, rather than be in need of editing and redacting in order to respect the oldest version of the Hebrew Scriptures extent, that is, the Septuagint. All in all, the amazing complementarity between the Septuagint and Hebrew that we have seen bespeaks some sort of constant awareness by the Jewish translators of a need to capture in Greek, as much as possible, the messianic concepts that would allow the larger Jewish community within the Roman Empire to immediately appreciate the marvelous fulfillment of a long expected savior, the messiah of God Jesus.

Selected Bibliography

Manuscripts

Harley 2838 (15th century)

Codex Sinaicitus (4th century)

Primary Sources

Anonymous. *The Odes Project: The Earliest Christian Hymnbook: The Odes of Solomon*. Translated by James Charlesworth. Eugene OR. Cascade Books, 2009

Anonymous. *The Old Testament Pseudepigrapha: Apocalyptic Literature and Testaments*, vol. 1. Edited by James Charlesworth. Garden City NY. Doubleday, 1983

Anonymous *[Protevangelium of James =]. The Infancy Gospel of James*. In *The Infancy Gospel of James and Thomas*. The Scholars Bible 2. Translated and edited by Robert Hock. 32-77. Santa Rosa CA. Polebrock, 1995

Athanasius of Alexandria. *Expositio in Psalmos*. Patrologia Graeca 27. Edited by Jean-Paul Migne. 59-590. Paris. J.-P. Migne, 1857

_____. *Works on the Spirit: Athanasius's Letters to Serapion on the Holy Spirit, and, Didymus's on the Holy Spirit*. Translated by A. Radde-Gallwitz and L. Ayres. Popular Patristics Series 43. Yonkers NY. St Vladimir's Seminary Press, 2011

Augustine of Hippo. *Of Holy Virginity*. In *St. Augustin: On the Holy Trinity, Doctrinal Treatises, Moral Treatises*, vol. 3. Edited by P. Schaff. Translated by C. L. Cornish. Buffalo, NY. Christian Literature Company, 1887

_____. *Tractates on the Gospel of John 11-27*. Edited by T.P. Halton. Translated by J.W. Rettig. Fathers of the Church 79. Washington DC. Catholic University of America Press, 2003

Ephrem the Syrian. *Commentary on Tatian's Diatesseron*, vol. 3. Downers Grove, IL. InterVarsity Press, 2005

Ephrem the Syrian (*graecus*). In Ὁσίου Ἐφραίμ τοῦ Σύρου ἔργα. Edited by K.G. Phrantzoles, vol. 6. Thessaloniki. To Perivoli tis Panagias, 1995

Ignatius of Antioch. *The Apostolic Fathers: Greek texts and English translations*. Translated by Michael Holmes. Grand Rapids. MI. Baker Books, 1999

Irenaeus of Lyons. *The Writings of Irenæus*, vol. 2. Edited by A. Roberts and J. Donaldson. Translated by A. Roberts and W. H. Rambaut. Edinburgh/London/Dublin. T. & T. Clark; Hamilton & Co.; John Robertson & Co, 1866

Jerome of Dalmatia. *Against Helvidius*. In *Jerome: Dogmatic and Polemic Works*. Edited by Hirmigild Dressler. Translated by John Hritzu. 3-46. The Fathers of the Church 31. Washington DC. Catholic University of America, 1981

_____. *Lives of Illustrious Men*. In *Theodoret, Jerome, Gennadius, Rufinus: Historical Writings, etc.*, vol. 3. Edited by Philip Schaff and H. Wace. Translated by Ernest Richardson. New York. Christian Literature Company, 1892

Justin Martyr. *Dialogue avec Trypon: Édition critique, traduction, commentaire*, vol. 1. Edited by Phillip Bobichon. Paradosis 47. Fribourg. University of Fribourg, 2003

John Chrysostom. *Saint Chrysostom: Homilies on the Acts of the Apostles and the Epistle to the Romans*, vol. 11. Edited by Phillip Schaff, J. Walker, et al. Translated by G. B. Stevens. New York. Christian Literature Company, 1889

Origen of Alexandria. *Ex Origenis commentariis in Psalmos. Patrologia Graeca* vol. 12. Edited by Jean Paul Migne. 1059-1686. Paris. J.-P. Migne, 1857

Modestus. *On the Dormition of Mary: Early Patristic Homilies*. Translated by Brian Daley. Popular Patristics Series 18. Crestwood, NY. St Vladimir's Seminary Press, 1998

Ps.-Maximus Confessor (John the Geometer). *The Life of the Virgin: Translated with an Introduction and Notes*. New Haven. Yale University Press, 2012

Tertullian. *Against Praxeas*. In *Latin Christianity: Its Founder, Tertullian*, vol. 3. Edited by A. Roberts, J. Donaldson, and A. C. Coxe. Translated by P. Holmes. Buffalo, NY. Christian Literature Company, 1885

Working Instruments

Aland, Kurt, M. Black, et al. (editors). *The Greek New Testament: Fourth Revised Edition (with Morphology)*. Stuttgart. Deutsche Bibelgesellschaft, 2006

Budd, Phillip. *The Word Bible Commentary: Numbers*. Waco TX. Word Biblical Commentaries, 1984

Geerard, M. (editor). *Corpus Christianorum Clavis Patrum Graecorum*, vol. 1. Turnhout: Brepols, 1983

Kittel, Rud, Paul Kahle, et al. (editors). *Biblia Hebraica Stuttgartensia*. Stuttgart. Deutsche Bibelstiftung, 1997

Kuo, Jason. *The Lexham Bible Dictionary*. Edited by J. D. Barry, D. Bomar, et al. Bellingham WA. Lexham Press, 2016

Liddell, Henry George, Robert Scott, and Henry Stuart Jones. *A Greek-English lexicon: With a revised supplement*. Oxford. Clarendon Press, 1996

Robinson, Maurice and William Pierpont (editors). *The New Testament in the Original Greek: Byzantine Text-Form 2018*. Nürnberg GE. VTR Publications, 2018

Thomas Aquinas. *Catena Aurea: Commentary on the Four Gospels*. Collected out of the Works of the Fathers: St. Luke. Edited by John H. Newman. Oxford. John Henry Parker, 1843

Weber, Robert, and Roger Gryson (editors). *Biblia sacra iuxta vulgatam versionem.* Stuttgart. Deutsche Bibelgesellschaft, 2007

Secondary Sources

Brock, Sebastian. "Fire from Heaven: From Abel's Sacrifice to the Eucharist: A Theme in Syriac Christianity." *Studia Patristica* 25 (1993): 229-243

Brown, Raymond. *Mary in the New Testament: A Collaborative Assessment by Protestant and Roman Catholic Scholars.* New York. Paulist Press, 1978

_____. *The Birth of the Messiah: A Commentary on the Infancy Narratives in the Gospels of Matthew and Luke.* 2nd edition. New York. London: Yale University Press, 1993

Brown, Raymond, Joseph Fitzmeyer and Ronald Murphy. *The Jerome Biblical Commentary,* 2 vols. Englewood Cliff NJ. Prentice Hall, 1968

Constas, Maximos. "The Story of an Edition: Antoine Wenger and John Geometres' *Life of the Virgin Mary.*" In *Marian Narratives in Texts and Images.* Edited by Thomas Arentzen and Mary Cunningham. 3-22. Cambridge: Cambridge University Press, 2019

Gieschen, Charles. *Angelomorphic Christology: Antecedents & Early Evidence.* Arbeiten zur Geschichte...42. Leiden. Brill, 1998

Jones, D. A. *Old Testament Quotations and Allusions in the New Testament.* Bellingham, WA. Logos Bible Software, 2009

Just, Arthur. *Luke,* vol. 3. Downers Grove IL. InterVarsity Press, 2005

Hirschauer, Emmanuel. "Origen's Interpretation of Lk 1:35: 'The Power of the Most High will Overshadow You.'" *Scrinium* 4 (2008): 32-44

Laurentin, René. *Présence de Marie: Histoire, spiritualité, fondements doctrinaux.* Paris. Salvator, 2011

Maunder, Chris. "Mary and the Gospel Narratives." In *The Oxford Handbook of Mary*. Edited by Chris Maunder. 21-39. Oxford: Oxford University Press, 2019

Nichols, Aidan. *There Is No Rose: The Mariology of the Catholic Church*. Minneapolis MN: Fortress Press, 2015

Troftgruben, T. M. *Luke as Historian*. In *The Lexham Bible Dictionary*. Edited by J. D. Barry, D. Bomar, et al. Bellingham WA. Lexham Press, 2016

Zerwick, Max, and Mary Grosvenor. *A grammatical analysis of the Greek New Testament*. Rome. Biblical Institute Press, 1974

About the Authors

Rev. Dr. Christiaan Kappes is currently academic dean and professor at Ss Cyril and Methodius Byzantine Catholic Seminary in Pittsburgh PA. He is author of numerous books and articles in peer-review publications that touch upon Mariology. Those who wish to study more formally with him or to obtain a Masters in Theology from his Theological School online should feel free to contact him at www.bcs.edu

William Albrecht is a Catholic Christian. He is an international speaker and debater. William is co-host for Reason & Theology, as well as having guest appeared on EWTN, Virgin Most Powerful Radio, and many other networks. William runs a website dedicated to the Early Church Fathers that includes unique translations, articles, commentaries, and debates on the Fathers of the Church. You can find out more about him on his website: www.PatristicPillars.com

Made in the USA
Coppell, TX
23 November 2024

40878927R00095